HUSH II

Breaking the Cycle of Silence
Around Sexual Abuse

AN ANTHOLOGY

TENITA C. JOHNSON

Published by So It Is Written, LLC
Detroit, MI
SoItIsWritten.net

Hush II: Breaking the Cycle of Silence Around Sexual Abuse
Copyright © 2021 by Tenita C. Johnson

Edited by: So It Is Written – www.SoItIsWritten.net

Formatting: Ya Ya Ya Creative – www.YaYaYaCreative.com

ISBN: 979-8-9850206-1-8

LCCN: 2021919883

PRINTED AND BOUND IN THE UNITED STATES OF AMERICA

Table of Contents

Visionary *Author* Statement
TENITA C. JOHNSON

"Don't say anything!"

"It's just our little secret!"

"If you love me, you won't tell. Keep this between us."

For years, boys and girls, men and women of all ages, all around the world, have heard these words. For many families, it's the elephant in the room that everyone chooses to ignore.

It's the reason why the kids can't go visit "Uncle James" or "Aunt Martha" anymore. Like a cancer, it oftentimes lies dormant and under the surface until it is triggered and simply can no longer be ignored.

Sexual abuse has been—and continues to be—a silent killer in our communities. While it may not kill someone physically, it has certainly killed years of joy and happiness, let alone one's peace. In a moment, it has killed the hopes and dreams of many whose lenses of life are now tainted. And because of the shame and the guilt, the hurt and the heartache, the voices of victims have been silenced for too many decades to count.

This is where the silence stops. This is where we give volume to the voices of victims who couldn't muster up the words to share their story. This is where we go back to get the little boy or girl who was touched inappropriately and been broken ever since. As a survivor of sexual abuse by both a man and a woman, I know firsthand how a seemingly short season of your life from childhood can literally propel you forward, or keep you stuck, once you're an adult. I also realize that a sure way for us to continue to overcome is by the blood of the lamb *and* by the word of our testimony.

Unfortunately, I was married with children of my own before I realized the impact that molestation had on my life. Intimacy with my husband has been, and sometimes continues to be, a challenge. If he touches me in a certain way, I jump. If he caresses a certain part of my body, my legs or arms may stiffen and lock up. No fault of his own, even the slightest touch can cause the largest trigger and cause me to shut down.

There are certain places my children simply cannot go. There are also certain children and family members we don't let visit our home. Our children can only spend the night or travel with select few friends or family. While I don't want to live in a continual state of panic, paranoia and fear, I don't want to be naïve or ignorant to the schemes of sexual predators either. My prayer and my hope are that this silent killer, and the long-term effects of it, stops with me. My prayer is that my children and their children, and even their children, won't have to endure the pain and agony of the aftermath of such a huge societal problem.

Sexual abuse knows no boundaries. It isn't only happening in the black community or the white community. It's not just happening to the poor and those who live in poverty-stricken communities. It's not just happening to little girls or women. Not all predators are men, and not all predators look the same. The moment we attempt to define the avatar of the "ideal sexual predator" is the moment that we lose focus on the problem at hand. Something so much larger, so much darker, is at work beneath the surface than the human beings we see committing these heinous acts. My mission is to shine a light on the root more than the symptoms of the problem—one that indeed may take me a lifetime to complete.

The views and opinions expressed in these stories are those of the authors. They do not necessarily reflect my personal views, nor the position of So It Is Written. Our experiences may be different. Our healing processes may be different. But, united, our vision, mission and purpose of this collaboration is the same: to give voice to the silent cries of victims of sexual abuse and move toward putting an end to this pandemic that continues to erode the effectiveness of the families in our communities, around the country and the world.

She touched me at the age of seven.

He touched me at the age of fourteen.

This is my story. This is *our* story. It's time to break the cycle of silence.

No More Closets
JERVIS CANTY

It's amazing how a simple touch can change the trajectory of a person's life. It can scar their perception of love and life. It can change their dreams and aspirations and challenge their very existence.

Sharing this story is one of the most difficult, yet freeing, things I have ever done in life. I've always tried my best to find a silver lining in all situations, even if it came at a cost to me and my own happiness and well-being. For years, I have carried the hurt, the pain, the guilt, the fault, and the memories of the events of my past that caused me to go within and hide from the realities of situations that took place in my life as a young child and teenager.

A touch from the wrong person, at the wrong time, too early, too late, can change the way you react to people and relationships. It can cause you to mistake the good for the bad.

Well, my story was affected by all of those previous emotions.

During an interview with Tenita Johnson for her podcast on male sexual abuse, I found myself facing one of life's greatest fears: telling the raw, unadulterated truth about what happened to me sexually at a young age.

Her first question was, "Who touched you?"

Hearing the question alone yielded a pain in my stomach. I felt like I could pass out or vomit at any given moment. I didn't know how to respond or react to the question with anything other than the truth.

My first touch came from a female cousin. She'd lay me on the sofa in front of her and fondle me. I had to be between the age of five and seven years old. This was the first of a few inappropriate touches and situations that would forever scar me and make me self-consciously label myself as a walking taboo. I also abhorred some really hard feelings. It was my first experience with sadness and depression. It was my first touch that I experienced but, unfortunately, it was not the last.

I'm sharing my story in hopes that it will not only free me completely from the traumas of my past, but also that it will help some other man—or woman—who may not have the courage to tell their story. It's time to confront your predators and find the strength to overcome the guilt of the past. You Are not guilty! You are not alone! You are *enough*!

Every young boy dreams of having his own money to buy whatever he wants, when he wants. All my life, as far back as I can remember, I've always had a passion for music. I loved listening to music and singing every song that came on the radio. I would record music on my cassette player and repeat it back until I learned every word and riff of every song. I used to sit on the front porch as a child and pretend I was Casey Kasem, the host of American Top 10, a music TV show in the 80s that would count down the top radio hits of the week every Saturday. I would watch it, then sit on the porch and imagine myself being the host. I counted down my favorite songs from ten, nine, eight…. all the way down to the number one song.

"And the number one song this week, moving up from Number 4, is *Hot Stuff* by Donna Summer!" Then, I'd play the song. Those were formative years for me. I don't remember ever being so happy in all my life. Music was always my safe place. One year, my mother bought a record player for my siblings and me for Christmas. I was excited to move from cassette tapes to actual records. In order to get the records for my countdown, I had to figure out a way to be able to buy 45 records (Yeah, I am telling my age here) for one dollar at the record store on the corner by my house. Mr. Dave ran the store, and he always sold me records for a dollar each. Then, he always gave me one record for free. But I had to figure out a way to get those records. My mom sometimes gave me money. But, as a single parent, she had to make every penny stretch.

My brother Kent (*May he RIP*) always seemed to have a hustle. That was something I always admired about him. Kent went from paper routes to cutting grass, amongst other things. He always found a way to get some money. Often, he asked me to go with him to cut grass. I wasn't always willing to go. Outside labor wasn't one of my things. He would borrow a neighbor's manual push lawnmower (*yep, manual lawnmower*) and go throughout the neighborhood, cutting grass. I finally agreed one day to go along. We went to about five different houses. While he cut the grass, he assigned me the task of raking the lawn and bagging up the grass. I hated it, but it was a way to get money. He got ten dollars, and he only gave me three—what a rip-off!

One particular day, we went to the house of a neighbor with whom we were very close for several reasons. He was related to a family member, which, in some way, made him family to us (*We'll call him Uncle Mitch for the sake of protecting the guilty*). He always paid the most money, which was $20 for cutting his lawn, front and back. We went to the house to cut the grass and he opened the garage so we could get the yard tools. He not only wanted the grass but the entire yard well-manicured. It took us longer to finish this yard because there was so much to do. But the payoff would be well worth it. After we were done, Kent collected the money and he split it in half with me. We continued to do this for quite a while every week and we were able to make good money. Eventually, Kent stopped cutting lawns because he started delivering newspapers. So, I kept cutting the lawns to make money—only now, I would get all of the money. I was so excited!

On my very first day, I went to cut Uncle Mitch's lawn. As usual, he opened the garage so I could get the tools. I was horrible at cutting the lawn, but I managed to pull it off. Uncle Mitch saw that I was struggling, so he came outside and helped a little. Finally, the lawn was all done. I put all the tools back in the garage, closed it, and went to the door to get paid. I was so excited to get that money.

Uncle Mitch opened the door and I followed him into the house. He was known for being a heavy drinker. When I entered the house, I could smell the alcohol on his breath immediately. We proceeded to the dining room.

"You want a pop?" he asked.

"Yes."

I drank my pop while he had a beer. I sat at the table and noticed that he had a lot of adult magazines spread out on the table. I was fourteen years old at the time. Seeing the magazines immediately made me nervous and excited at the same time. It had to show on my face because Uncle Mitch responded immediately.

"It's okay. You want to see them?" he asked.

I took him up on his offer. As I looked through the magazine, I became aroused and erect, but I remained seated so Uncle Mitch wouldn't see my erection through my shorts. Uncle Mitch disappeared into the den as I continued looking through the magazines. He came out of the room shortly after, wearing a white undershirt and white underwear. I saw it, but I have to admit, it didn't make me nervous or scared. He sat down at the table across from me, grabbed another beer, and joined me as I continued flipping through the magazines. I looked up and noticed that Uncle Mitch was fondling and pleasuring himself.

"You want to take your clothes off, too? I'm sure they're dirty from cutting the grass," he said.

I obliged and removed all of my clothing, except my underwear.

"Are you hard?" he asked.

"Yes."

"I can't believe how big you are. Have you ever "jacked off" before?"

"I don't know what you mean."

In that moment, he stood up. His underwear was completely off, and I was able to see his fully erect penis as he took it in his hand and pleasured himself yet again. At this point, I was still calm and, honestly, intrigued.

Suddenly, he stopped and walked back into the den. But he left the door open this time. He asked me to join him in the room, and I got up and followed him. As we got into the room, I noticed he had the television on with porn playing on the television. I sat on the sofa across from the television. I felt embarrassed and now nervous at this point because I was completed fascinated by the porn on the television—something I had never seen in my life. I was completely erect after seeing this. But still, I stood in place.

Uncle Mitch told me, "Relax. Do you like what you see?"

I replied, "A little bit."

"Sit down."

I sat on the sofa on the opposite end of him.

"You want to remove your underwear?" he asked.

I nervously said, "No." But he encouraged me that it was okay to take it off.

As we sat on the sofa, Uncle Mitch continued to pleasure himself as I watched the porn scene in amazement. This was my first time watching porn. I honestly was drawn to it.

"Watch me and do what I'm doing," he said.

Fear came over me. This was all so new for me. But I did what he asked and began to pleasure myself. It honestly felt good to me in spite of the fact that I was really nervous and shaking. My body was experiencing a pleasure I had never experienced before.

I gave in to it.

As I continued to watch the porn, and do what Uncle Mitch did, Uncle Mitch adjusted himself on the sofa. He was now laying with his head toward me, close to my lap. I can't remember if I stopped pleasuring myself or not. But I do remember him telling me to put my penis in his mouth.

I said, "No!"

Again, he reminded me that it was okay for me not to be nervous. He told me I could continue "jacking off" by myself, so I did. As I continued, he started rubbing my leg. I am sad to say, it felt good to me. I let him as he laid on his stomach facing me. Once again, he told me to relax. He was calm, so I relaxed.

He touched my penis and eventually started performing oral sex on me. Soon, I ejaculated. His demeanor suddenly changed. He jumped up off the sofa and yelled at me.

"Why did you cum?"

I was immediately afraid because I didn't know what I had done wrong to make him yell at me. My feelings were really hurt at this point. I felt like I had done everything he wanted me to and, yet, he was angry at me. He went into the bathroom and handed me a washcloth. He demanded that I clean myself up and also clean up his sofa. When he did, I hurriedly put on my underwear and continued to clean up the mess I had made. I never placed the blame on him. This later became a horrible habit for me: taking the blame for things that I shouldn't have. I had done as he had demanded, yet, I was being disciplined for doing it. When he returned from the bathroom a second time, he walked over to me and grabbed me by my arm. He demanded me to look him in the eyes. By this time, I had tears in my eyes out of fear, embarrassment and shame.

He told me very angrily, "You better not tell anybody what happened! If you do, I'm going to kill your mother."

I left the house feeling so many emotions I was unable to deal with in that moment. I was ashamed because it happened. I was embarrassed because I had these feelings. I wasn't sure if they were right or wrong. I felt afraid because I wasn't able to tell anybody. I wouldn't have wanted to tell anybody anyway because of the shame. I left questioning, *Why did this happen? More than anything else, what would happen to my mom?* I was so afraid of what was next for me.

It seemed like it took me forever to get home, which was only two streets over from Uncle Mitch's house. When I finally got home, I found myself crying. I didn't want anyone to know. My mom had the front door opened. Instead of coming in the house and going to the bathroom, or to my room, I went into the coat closet and sat there. I was so sad, scared and overwhelmed. I sat there in the closet and cried quietly. That closet seemed like the safest place in the world for me. As I sat in the closet, I remember scaring my mother because she opened the closet to return something to the closet and she saw me.

She asked, "Why are you in the closet?"

I told her, "I don't feel well."

She reached out and gave me the biggest hug. I told her I was going to bed, and I did just that. There was no way I could tell her about my experience. I didn't want her to be hurt by Uncle Mitch. This was one of the hardest moments of anybody's life—and it happened to be mine.

Uncle Mitch called the house the following week and asked me to cut his grass again. I was so afraid to go. But I remembered his words that were now engraved in my head. I went to his house to cut his grass again, only to find myself in the same position. But, this time, there were no threats. There were more elevated experiences with Uncle Mitch forcing himself on me, forcing oral sex on me and eventually forcing me to have oral sex with him. It never got to penetration. This continued for the remainder of that summer. The following summer, I wasn't able to go back and cut the grass because I had a summer job with the Summer Youth Program. This ended that experience with Uncle Mitch. I was so glad, but it didn't take away the guilt or fear. I was relieved that it wasn't going to happen again.

Unfortunately, that was a far cry from the truth.

I unfortunately was gang raped the following summer by some others I didn't know on the way to school. This drove me deeper into depression and despair. I felt like this was my fate.

In my late twenties, I got the news that Uncle Mitch had passed away. I couldn't feel any emotions at the time, but I do remember being asked to sing a song for his funeral. I declined. I never explained why, and, by God's grace, I was never asked why.

From these experiences, I was uncomfortable being around boys and men. I never really had many male friends. But after that, it made me withdraw from the few I had. It made me fearful in my dealings with other people. I was never one to have dealings with a lot of people. Although I was very popular in high school, I was very shy and guarded.

As an adult, I later joined a support group for women of sexual abuse—here were no male groups at that time to attend. I didn't know I'd get torn apart by women who felt I should not be a part of the group. They were violated by men, so they didn't feel safe with a man joining the group. Needless to say, I only attended the initial meeting and never returned. I felt less than from the pains and abuses of my past. Now, I was being torn down by women. They didn't care that I had gone through the same level of hurt and abuse as them. This caused me to become a pain hoarder. I kept all of my pains and hurts to myself because I didn't want to be a burden on others. I didn't trust anyone enough to share my deepest feelings and hurts because I felt they wouldn't understand. I knew they would judge me instead of helping or saving me.

I questioned if I was a *real* man or not. I questioned if I was ever enough. I became so consumed and engrossed in everyone else's feelings that I masked mine and avoided being too close to them. I felt like they would abuse me. I inflicted my internal traumas upon myself.

I later attempted suicide.

I would self-sabotage any experiences that made me happy. I bared the weight of guilt for everything, whether I it was guilty or not.

One thing about abuse is that it doesn't discriminate. It doesn't care or protect. It hurts you. And if you're not careful, it will make you hurt yourself and even others around you. I am blessed to say that I worked hard at healing. I am truly healing all of my relationships. I am careful about the way I treat others. I am also careful about how I allow others to treat me. I protect Jervis. I love Jervis. I honor and commend Jervis for being strong and surviving.

It wasn't easy at all, but it was worth every tear. I hope that my story can help heal, you, your children, your spouse, your friends, and more importantly, yourself.

I often ask myself if I'll ever be completely healed from my past hurts. I now say, "One day at a time. But no more closets!"

Breaking the Cycle of Silence

Reflection Questions

1. What would you do to protect yourself from being hurt by your past?

    _____

    _____

    _____

    _____

    _____

2. Where was your hiding place after you were hurt and didn't want to face anyone?

    _____

    _____

    _____

    _____

    _____

3. What messages are you giving to your family and loved ones to let them know they can trust you with those "harsh reality" moments? What messages are you giving yourself that you can, too?

    _____

    _____

    _____

    _____

    _____

    _____

    _____

4. How have the events of your past altered your visions and dreams of your future?

    _____

    _____

    _____

    _____

    _____

5. What would you tell you violators if you knew then what you know now?

_____

_____

_____

_____

_____

ABOUT THE AUTHOR

---===⟨⟩===---

Jervis Canty

Jervis Canty is the Host and Producer of *JERVIS CANTY & FRIENDS: AT HOME EDITION*, an award-winning virtual talk show/podcast streaming live weekly on Facebook. Jervis has interviewed many local and national figures, such as: Richard Smallwood, Beverly Crawford, Anita Wilson, Cocoa Brown, Chrisette Michele, Percy Bady, Lynne Fiddmont, Lynette Hawkins-Stephens, Maysa Leak, and many more. He is the writer and creator of the hit self-written and produced stage play, *When Loving You Is Hurting Me*, for which he was honored with his several award nominations and is awaiting the opportunity to present his second follow up stage plays, *Loves Hangover: After Loves Hurt and Club Chronicles*.

As an actor, he has toured with *Murder at Carver High 20 Year Class Reunion* (Mr. Watkins) with *Mystique Dinner Shows* and *Gotta Love Ya till I Die* (Redd Foxx) to name a few. He also contributed to various film and television projects, including Comedy Central's, *Detroiters*, and Principal Television Commercial Roles for *District Detroit*

(Detroit Pistons), ASPCA, as well as Kellogg. Jervis is also a self-taught graphic designer, among his many other talents.

Pre-pandemic, Jervis has also hosted various shows including his self-titled, *Saturday Night Live w/Jervis Canty & Friends Series* at Aretha's Jazz Café, as well as various other projects including his former radio show with *WGOD Radio* entitled, *Entrepreneurs of Detroit w/Jervis Canty*. Jervis is working on the release of his first book project coming very soon. Jervis is proud to be a founding member of the *Kyren Anthony-Rose Jamison Foundation*, a 501c3 organization whose mission is to provide financial relief and assistance to cover funeral costs to families who have experienced the sudden loss of a stillborn or child within the first three years of life. The *Jervis Canty and Friends* Podcast has won multiple awards, including 2nd Place in the WDIV (Channel 4 Detroit) VOTE 4 THE BEST Favorite Podcast, 2021 KRAVE HONORS Hidden Gem Award, the Spirit of Detroit Award from the Detroit City Council, and the 2021 Detroit Choice Award for Favorite Podcast.

For more information on Jervis and
any upcoming events and efforts, follow him on the
Jervis Canty and Friends Facebook Group page or
email jerviscantyandfriends@gmail.com.

Suffering in Silence
MIRACLE NORED

This dude swore he was Too Short. He was pill popping, pimping and drinking pints of liquor. That's how he got down on a daily basis. He was known for selling drugs and "punani" (a nickname for a vagina). If you left something valuable unattended in his presence, it was as good as gone. Then, he would lie about it straight in your face, with a strong conviction as the nerve in his bottom lip started twitching.

I was seven years old when this Too Short wannabe and his friends came over to play cards and have a few drinks before it was time to go back to the YMCA for lockdown.

"It's getting late," Tookie said to my mom. "We gone head on out."

When they left, my mom went with her friend down the street. She told me and my oldest brother to go to bed. Shortly after, we woke up to a window being broken and men's voices. We hid under the bed. We heard someone say, "Come on, man! Let's go! She is coming right back!"

Soon after, my mom came in. We had been robbed. My mom was furious, but she knew Tookie was responsible for this. The next day, Tookie came over like nothing happened. When my mom told him what happened, his bottom lip got to twitching. He seemed shocked and even offered support. I could tell my mom thought he was responsible for the break-in, but she did not have any proof. So, she left it alone.

We did not see Tookie for years after that incident. He was in and out of jail for pimping, drugs or domestic violence.

The next time Tookie came back around was shortly after my father had molested me. Tookie and my father did not really get along, mainly because they were a lot alike. My father was an alcoholic, and abusive to my mom, my siblings and myself. One night, my mom and dad were arguing. It didn't take much for my dad to get angry. But this time, Tookie was there, and he stood up for my mom. When he asked my mom if she wanted him gone, Tookie forced my dad to leave. Now as much as we didn't trust Tookie, he became our hero that night. Soon, he came around every day. One day, me and Tookie were playing *I Declare War* and we had a conversation about my dad.

"What happened between you and your dad?"

"What you mean?"

"You seemed different around him, like he had done something wrong to you?"

"Ummm, no. I just don't like him."

"Now, you know you can trust me. Whatever we talk about is between us. You my favorite cuz, and I won't let nothing happen to you."

"If I tell you, you gotta promise not to say anything because momma made me promise not to talk about it again."

"Lil cuz, you don't have nothing to worry about."

"One night, momma was gone and me and my siblings was home with my dad. We were up watching TV. Dad came and put a tape in the VCR. He said, 'Since we're up, we can all watch TV together.' I remember thinking, *My mom is going to really be mad that dad had us watching pornography*. I was feeling very uncomfortable. I could tell by the look on my brother's and sister's faces that they were uncomfortable as well. Shortly after, dad told my siblings to go to bed and shut the door. At this point, I went from being uncomfortable to downright scared. My dad asked me what type of body I wanted to have when I got older. I sat there, quiet and shaking, as he pointed out breasts on other women. He asked me, "Do you want your breasts to look like theirs?"

With tears running down my face, I asked, "Can I please go to bed?"

He replied angrily, "Yeah! Get the hell out of here."

With great relief, I jumped up and started heading to the bedroom that my sister and I shared. He stopped me in my tracks and yelled at me.

"Where the hell are you going? You are sleeping in my bed tonight."

I started crying harder. I begged him to let me sleep with my sister.

He screamed again. "Girl, get yo behind in that room before I beat the mess out of you!"

I was so afraid that I just did what he said. I went in the room and wrapped myself in the blanket like a swaddled baby. I hoped he would get so drunk and simply go to sleep. As I laid there for what seemed like hours, I kept replaying what had just happened. I couldn't believe it. I thought I was in a bad nightmare and simply couldn't wake up. A little time had passed, and it was quiet. I got ready to turn over to try to get some sleep when I heard him walking toward the door. He came in and told me to undress.

I said, "Daddy, why? I don't want to take my clothes off!"

He said, "Girl, take your clothes off! I'm your dad and I should know your body better than any other nigga!"

"Daddy, please! I just want to go to sleep!"

He yelled, "Girl, take them damn clothes off now. Don't make me say it again."

I guess I wasn't moving fast enough, so he started fondling me underneath my clothes. I laid there, frozen in fear. I was too scared to scream out loud, but I was surely screaming on the inside. He touched me in ways that a father is not supposed to touch their child, then just left the house. Although there was no penetration, I felt violated, damaged, scared, angry, confused. So many thoughts and feelings were going through my mind and body.

When my mom came home, I ran to her, crying. I could tell from the look on her face that she knew something had happened. When I told her what happened, she became furious. She confronted him with so much rage. For the first time in my life, I saw my mom stand up to my dad. But, of course, he told her I was lying. He told her I was making things up. I saw the rage decrease and turn to sadness. My mother's rage turned to fear as my father defended himself with anger, deception and intimidation.

"I knew that mother sucker did something! That's why she said she wanted him to leave."

"Yep. I think so, too. You kind of saved us from the monster."

"I would kill that nigga if he tried some mess like that again, grinning with his bottom lip twitching."

After that conversation, me and Tookie bonded. He was the cool, big cousin. He was really my momma's first cousin. I started babysitting for one of his women when he took her out in the streets to make money. One day, he asked my mom if I could babysit for one of the women at his house. It was easy money for the summer and my mom didn't mind. So, I went. Tookie and his woman came back in arguing after Tookie had jumped on her badly. She got her kids and left. Tookie wasn't driving, so he had to call my mom and tell her he'd get me home tomorrow.

He gave me a blanket and told me to sleep on the couch. I remember praying, "Lord, please protect me! Don't let what happened to me before happen to me again." I wrapped myself tightly in the blanket and finally went to sleep.

I went home the next morning. Two weeks later, the dust had settled over the argument and fighting between Tookie and his girlfriend, so I started babysitting again. Except, this time, he called and asked my mom if I could come baby sit—but when I got there, no kids were home.

"Where is everyone at?" I asked.

"They should be here soon," he said.

Before I knew it, I had fallen asleep on the couch. I didn't wake up until about 11 p.m. I asked Tookie if he could just take me home. Instead, he agreed to take me first thing in the morning. I didn't think twice about. I laid back down and fell asleep.

Unfortunately, I was awakened out of my sleep by Tookie taking my pants off.

"What are you doing?" I yelled. "Stop, Tookie! Stop! Please don't do this!"

I cried. I tried to resist by holding my pants as much as I could, but he was too strong. He grabbed my wrist and twisted it really hard.

He told me, "Shut the heck up before I beat your behind like you stole something! You gave it to your daddy! Now you gone give me this young punani! You know you want it. I bet that punani tight and right."

"Please stop! Please stop! I'm telling my momma!"

But he wouldn't listen. He slapped me and said, "Say something else! I double dog dare you!"

By this time, he had taken my pants off and forced himself in me. The pain I was feeling, and the fear I had, had me in a frozen state. I couldn't move. I couldn't say anything else. I just laid there until it was over.

"Go clean yo self up!" he yelled at least three times. But I was in such a state of shock that I couldn't respond. So, he grabbed me and yelled, "Go clean up, I said!"

I ran to the bathroom with my pants in my hand and sat on the bathroom floor crying.

"Hurry up out of there!" he yelled.

When I stood, there was a puddle of blood on the floor. I cleaned myself up, came out of the bathroom and asked if I could go home. Tookie noticed the blood on the bathroom floor.

"What the heck was you in here doing? This is all your fault!"

He put his hands around my neck and choked me. He said, "If you say anything to anybody, I'll kill your mom and siblings."

I was gasping for breath as he asked me if I understood. I nodded my head affirmatively.

"Now, go lay on the couch and stop that crying before I beat yo behind. You a woman now, so act like it."

As I laid there, I was thinking of ways I could leave without him knowing. I had to get to my mom before he did and tell her what happened. Maybe I could run to a neighbor's house and call the police. I came up with a lot of good ideas. But honestly, I was afraid to do anything. My father was the biggest monster in the world to me, and Tookie had got rid of him. I'd seen him beat women whom he claimed he loved, so I knew he was capable of doing everything he said he would. I made up my mind that I was never saying anything to anyone about what happened. After all, when my father molested me, nothing happened to him. I had to live with him for years even after I told. In my mind, this would be no different. I decided I wasn't saying a word to anyone ever in my life. This was something I had planned to take to my grave.

The next morning, Tookie took me home. Before I got out the car, he grabbed the back of my neck and said, "Don't forget what I told you. I will kill you and no one would believe you anyway. I'll tell everyone that you told me you lied on your dad to get him out of the house and your mom will put you in a girls' home."

"I won't say nothing. I promise." I got out of the car.

I thought my nightmare was over, but it wasn't. It happened again and again. Each time, he put a gun to my head, and told me to take my clothes off and lay there. So, I did.

In freeze mode.

Feeling numb.

Afraid and hopeless each time.

At this point, I didn't even waste my time resisting. Although I didn't want it to happen, he never listened to me.

So, I just hushed!

We hadn't seen Tookie in a month or so and, honestly, I was happy. But I was even happier when my mom told me he had gone out of town and was arrested. He would be gone for a while. The big, bad wolf was gone. I released a sound of relief.

A few weeks later, I started feeling sick and throwing up all the time. An older friend of mine said, "Girl, you're probably pregnant!" and she burst out laughing. Then, she said, "Naw! Yo butt still a virgin. You might just have the flu or something." I sat there quietly, thinking about the past few months of my life and everything that had happened. I indeed was a virgin before my virginity was stolen from me. I cried so hard.

Yolanda yelled, "Miracle, what's wrong?"

I wiped my face and said, "Nothing. I'm good." I simply went home.

The next day, all I could think about was what she said: "You could be pregnant!" How could I tell my mom I might be pregnant? I'd never been with a guy or been seen with a guy. I tried to get up the nerve to her the truth, thinking, *Maybe I can tell her since he is locked up. Maybe we could press charges and he would get more time.* But the fear overrode my nerve to say anything.

So, I became promiscuous. I hung around guys in the neighborhood. Before I knew it, my good-girl name was tarnished. Slowly, rumors spread about me in the neighborhood. It was strange how everyone believed the rumors, and no one even asked me about the change in my behavior. I guess what caused me to start acting this way didn't matter.

Shortly after, I found out I was pregnant. I'd never even willingly had sex. Now I was pregnant. I couldn't tell momma what happened. I was scared to tell anyone anything at this point. I felt like if I told someone else, it was going to happen to me again. So, I started hanging out with this older guy so people in the neighborhood could put a face to the pregnancy when I started showing. I even had sex with him and acted like I was a virgin so I could tell him it was his baby. I know that was wrong, but I was fifteen years old and scared for my life. I was desperate to keep what happened to me from the world. I don't know what I was more scared of: Tookie making good on his promise or telling someone else, and they take that as permission to rape me again. So, I kept quiet. Every time I thought about telling someone the truth, I told myself, "Hush!" When my mom asked who the father of the baby was, I wanted to tell her the truth. I wanted to tell her what happened so everyone would know I wasn't just this fass little girl. I was forced to be this way to survive. I told her his name was Toran, the older guy I had been hanging out with in the neighborhood.

I was so humiliated being pregnant at fifteen. I had to live with being talked about, treated indifferently and suffering in silence from the baggage left to me after I was molested by my father and raped and impregnated by my mother's cousin. Before all of this, I was a virgin and I had good grades in school. They stole my innocence. They took away my self-esteem. They took away my identity. In order to get through this pregnancy, I had to become the promiscuous little girl I appeared to be. I would have rather dealt with the humiliation and shaming than to tell someone what had really happened to me. I feared for my life. I feared it would happen again. I even started blaming myself. I thought, *Did I do something that attracted these monsters to me?*

So, I stop caring about how I looked. I no longer wanted to be a girly girl. I wanted to hide within myself, so no one ever saw me. No one would want to take anything away from me again.

Maybe a year after giving birth to my son, I think Toran figured out it wasn't his baby. The rumor was that I had slept with so many people that I didn't know who the father was. The humiliation didn't stop. The pain wouldn't go away. I became a prisoner of my emotions, still suffering in silence.

I tried to commit suicide.

The mental torment of what happened, coupled with the lies being told about me, was too much to bear. Although I didn't really want to die, I just didn't want to feel this pain anymore that I couldn't tell anyone about.

Thank God, I survived it. Since I survived it, I might as well get over it, so I can live. So, I did. I went on for years, not remembering a thing about it, completely dissociating myself from the events. I suppressed the pain—until I was triggered years later.

My father was around, but I was grown by then. I only dealt with him when it was beneficial to me and, most times, he was watching my kids. He never went all the way with me. I'd told my mom and we never heard about him doing anything like this again. I assumed he wouldn't try anything with my children. I was so focused on having a babysitter that I didn't allow myself to think about what he had done to me.

What I do know is that, one night, he was watching my kids. When I came home, I felt something had happened and I flipped out terribly. I was so messed up because of everything I had been through. I was masking the pain and trying to fill voids that had been missing for so long by someone who finally gave me the sense of protection that I was longing for as a child. However, I was failing as a parent in protecting my own children. I was focused on getting the very things I was missing as a child that I was willing to leave my children in several situations that were not safe. At that time, I didn't think twice about it. I didn't realize how messed up I was. I didn't realize I was still living life based on who I had pretended to be when I was trying to survive. Shortly after, I decided I need to change my life. I wanted to be a better mother and a better human overall. I started going to church and trying to live my life like the church people said I should.

Things were finally starting to change for the better. It seems like I've been through hell and high water since the sexual abuse that started when I was only thirteen. My oldest son came due to the sexual abuse from the hands of Tookie, when I was about fifteen years old. I started my journey of healing from within. I had a whole lot of trauma and childhood adverse experience to unpack. I was finally ready to face the reality of my past. Thankfully, I was able to have an open, honest conversation with him about what he did to me and what I thought may have happened to my children. I still don't know. I think I blocked it out of my mind completely.

Here is how the conversation went as I was driving him home one night.

"Dad, I need to talk to you about something."

"What, baby girl? Go ahead. I'm listening."

"I have hated you my entire life. You were supposed to protect me. You were supposed to love me and be the good example of how a man is supposed to treat a woman. But you weren't. Instead, you were a monster. You taught me to be afraid of men. You taught me to be afraid to express my anger because I didn't want to lose it like you did and become abusive to my children. You were supposed to protect my innocence, but you stole it from me. I blame you for every time I was sexually abused because you got away with it. I didn't feel my voice had power, so I suffered in silence every time I was sexually abused."

"I know, baby girl. I did get away with it. My life has been a living hell for how I lived my life, and I'm still paying for it. I took how you would disrespect me, and only deal with me if I was giving you money or doing something you needed because I didn't deserve anything more from you. I'm sorry, baby girl. I'm sorry for what happened. I'm sorry for the pain I caused you. Please forgive me."

"I forgive you, Dad. I want you to come to church with me. The pastor was teaching about forgiveness, and it helped me to really forgive you."

That conversation was the most meaningful conversation I ever had with my dad. Later, he started going to church with me, drunk and all. He gave his life to God and was baptized. Shortly after, we found out he had stage four cancer. I insisted that he stay with me in hospice care so I could take care of him.

I did just that until he made his transition.

I hadn't heard from or seen Tookie in years. Then, one day, I was watching the news. I'd heard that a man who was stealing copper out of an abandoned house was severely injured when the house collapsed on him. I later found out that it was Tookie, and he was in a coma. I felt nothing. No happiness. No joy. No relief. No *nothing*. Days later, at a church event, a friend of mine shared her testimony regarding an experience that reminded me of what happened to me with Tookie. She shared how she went to the hospital and forgave a person who was in a coma. Then, I had urges to go visit him.

While he was in the coma, I told him who I was. I told him that I forgave him and that I prayed while he still had a chance, that he would ask God to forgive him. No matter how he lived his life, if he asked for forgiveness, and accepted

Jesus Christ as his Lord and Savior, he would be forgiven. I knew God would give him eternal life. Then, I left. I felt so relieved. So much pressure was released from me.

Days later, he passed away. I had to take my mom to the funeral. I honestly thought I was going to be okay. But as the funeral director spoke, tears started falling from my face. The negative emotions were overwhelming, and I was trying to push them back. I was trying to think about something else. But, for thirty minutes or so, I was that scared teenager again. I was terrified and in so much pain. Then, I heard a still, small voice telling me, "You're safe to process the pain and be free!"

So, I took a deep breath. As I exhaled, I allowed myself to face the reality of what happened to me. I allowed myself to feel the pain and release the fear. Finally, the tears stopped. The teenager within me who had been raped and physically abused for months, threatened daily, and filled with fear was being restored and free from that emotional and mental prison of my past. I felt so much peace, and a calmness came upon me. Even though I had so much breakthrough from the sexual abuse with both my father and Tookie, I realized that I still had more work to do.

The two men in my life who were supposed to protect me betrayed my trust. I suffered unknowingly for a while with betrayal trauma, never trusting anyone. I often held on to a very unhealthy relationship with a man simply because he protected me. I didn't realize that it was the teenager inside of me who longed for this protection. The more my relationship with God, and the Word of God, developed, the more I realize I needed to get out of this toxic relationship that was damaging me and my children. I did, but it wasn't easy because unhealthy soul ties and trauma bonding is real. It causes you to accept things you shouldn't accept. I honestly never had a chance to really recover from everything I went through and get to know *the real, authentic me.*

Any time the man I was with at the time talked about foreplay as part of sex, I immediately turned off. It wasn't until I was married in 2015 that I really noticed it. Every time my husband talked sexually to me, I immediately turned off and our sex life was hindered in the very beginning because of the sexual abuse. When I took myself through a series of questions to understand why my body was responding this way to my husband, I realized that I was being triggered by him talking about sex. That was what each abuser did before they sexually abused me.

So, when I realized this, I had a choice to make. I could either take responsibility and deal with this issue so it no longer hindered my marriage, or I could let it continue triggering me, act like nothing was wrong and watch my marriage suffer. I decided to deal with it the way I would coach my clients to deal with their trauma. Whenever I was triggered by my husband, I would coach myself through the trigger. I told myself, "I'm okay. It's safe. This is my husband and it's okay for him to talk to me this way."

I survived it, and now I have a very healthy sex life with a man who honors my body and respects me when I decline intimacy. I had to spend time rewiring my brain to respond differently when I'm triggered and safe. Even though I wasn't mentally remembering what happened, my body kept record of the experience and my mind couldn't separate the past from the present.

Because of the sexual abuse, my marriage was also burdened by my paranoia. My baby boy was eight years old when we were married. Our bedroom was upstairs. Every time my husband went downstairs to use the restroom at night, I would tiptoe behind him and listen to make sure he didn't go in my son's room. My husband couldn't even go and talk to my son in his room when it was dark. I would freak out. I realized that I was living in fear of it happening to my son. Since I had failed at protecting my children before, I was determined to protect my youngest child. My intentions were right, but they were rooted in fear. So, I wasn't handling it properly. I knew I had to change. I had to regain a sense of safety and trust with my husband, even though he never did any harm to me or cause me not to trust him. I just had to open up to my husband about everything that happened to me so he could at least understand the reason for my madness. I let him know that if my son or grandchild ever told me that he touched or talked to them inappropriately, nothing nice would follow.

I also had a talk with my son and explained to him what happened to me. I explained that I didn't want anything to happen to him. I encouraged him never to do anything he felt uncomfortable doing. I told him that if anyone ever did or said anything sexual or made him feel uncomfortable, he needed to come to me and tell me. I also told him if he didn't feel comfortable telling me to tell somebody in authority to tell me. I explained to him it didn't matter who it was, family or not. I would believe him and protect him. it took some time, but I'm no longer being negatively controlled by the fear of my son being sexually abused. I'm cautious, but not controlled. Every opportunity I get to teach him about the different forms of sexual abuse, I do.

Not wanting to deal with the sexual abuse issues in my family, and the fear of what others thought, hindered me tremendously. I kept silent when I should have spoken up. Because I was too much of a coward back then to confront or deal with this issue for what it was, or what I thought it was, it caused my kids to suffer. Now I'm on a mission as a trauma recovery coach to help people (including my children) to win from within. The steps that I took as I started the road to recovery in my own life are the steps that I repeat as needed. Prayerfully, these steps will jumpstart your road to recovery as well.

1. Decide to take ownership of your life. No more blaming people for where you are or making excuses for your current behavior. You're not responsible for what happened to you, but you are responsible for your recovery.

2. Face the reality of what happened. It happened. It hurt. They disappointed you. They didn't protect you or they did harm to you in some kind of way. Give yourself permission to feel the pain.

3. Forgive them. Forgiveness is for you, whether they ask for the forgiveness or not. Holding unforgiveness is like holding yourself hostage to the pains of your past and waiting on the person who hurt you to pay the ransom. Jesus has already paid their debt and yours. Forgive.

4. Give yourself permission to be authentically you. Separate what happened to you from who you were created to be. You are not the bad experiences that happened to you. You are not the mistakes you

made. You are not the negative picture that others have painted of you. You are fearfully and wonderfully made to win from within and show up as your authentic self!

Breaking the Cycle of Silence
Reflection Questions

1. What about this story resonates with you most, and why?

    _____

    _____

    _____

    _____

    _____

2. What "Ah Ha" moment have you had in connecting the dots
    from your past to your present?

    _____

    _____

    _____

    _____

    _____

3. When was the first time you experienced betrayal trauma and how has this hindered your relationships?

_____

_____

_____

_____

_____

4. What role does forgiveness play in your life?

_____

_____

_____

_____

_____

5. What can you do to reconcile your past mistakes?

_____

_____

_____

_____

_____

ABOUT THE AUTHOR

Miracle Nored

From the lost and abused, to the broken and the brokenhearted, Miracle Nored strategically uses her platform in ministry, coaching and business to break the mental and emotional barriers that hinder people from showing up as their authentic selves and empowering them to triumph externally through internal transformation. As an advocate for sexual abuse and mental illness, author, speaker and certified Trauma Recovery Coach, Miracle Nored is on a mission to help others eradicate emotional strongholds and mental bondage preventing them from living a life of abundance.

With a degree in Business Management from Wayne County Community College, Miracle serves as Co-Owner of Nored Services alongside her husband, Paul Nored. She is also a Certified Professional Life Coach of Building Beyond Barriers, where she offers one-on-one and group coaching, mental health first-aid certification and workshops.

In addition to being an ordained minister, Miracle's experience as a successful business owner, intercessor and licensed minister further positions her as a leader in ministry and the marketplace. She is best known for transforming lives through the power of prayer, her personal testimony with transparency, and her determination to see other people free from the private prisons of their past pain.

Trained in trauma informed care, biblical counseling, inner healing and certified as a mental health first aid instructor, Miracle continues to be a beacon of hope and light to those she encounters daily.

Stay connected with Miracle:

Fb: miraclenored

www.coachmiraclenored.com

Consent Without Comprehension
HOY MONK II

Before I start my story, I want to honor my Ma for being an awesome and amazing mom. I couldn't have prayed for a better Ma. This story is in no way a fault of my Ma, nor should she receive any condemnation from it. My Ma always taught me that if anyone touched me, I should tell her.

I never told her until I was in my early 30s. But as a male, society, family and friends (even women) will tell you that it's okay for an older woman or girl to touch a boy. In fact, it's looked at as a badge of honor. You are shunned or called names if you say anything if your predator, rapist or offender is a woman or girl. There are many parents who don't know their children were molested, sexually abused and/or raped until later in life. Some would rather take it to the grave than tell their parents. A lot of times, there is the fear of what one's parents may say or how will they respond. There are so many scenarios that play in the mind of the one who has been harmed sexually by someone else.

I truly believe God needs to be included. God needs to control the situation when the conversation happens. God is the only one who can control anything. *Anything*. But I believe the conversation needs to be had. I am extremely confident that my story is one of millions for males. By sharing my story, I'm not looking for pity, reparations, sympathy or attention. I'm hoping to bring light to a narrative that has been created for males who have been taught to just toughen up and take it. It's no big deal. It doesn't hurt that bad. It can't be that bad. A narrative that tells us we can't show emotion because we are weak if we do. A narrative that says it's okay for an older woman or girl to touch you inappropriately because it's the opposite sex and you should strive to sleep with older girls and women anyway. I only listed a few narratives. You mix these narratives in with the constant suppression of boys' and men's feelings and emotions, and you get what we have seen forever. There are a lot of men who don't know how to effectively show emotion, express feelings and be vulnerable with trusted people.

My incident happened when I was about six or seven years old. Some parts are very vivid, while others are blacked out and gapped. I never noticed this about myself before. But in telling this experience, I have learned something new about myself. Something that was always there, but I simply never paid attention to it. I learned that, in traumatic situations that happened to me as a child, I blacked out certain parts. I came to notice this because I recalled other traumatic scenarios from my childhood. I remember them the same way, bits and pieces and blacked out moments. Maybe God was blocking out certain parts to protect me. Or maybe I blocked them out because they were too traumatic, and I didn't want to remember them. It could have been both God and me. Either way, whether it was God protecting me by blocking pieces of my trauma, or it was me blocking those same pieces out, I'm grateful. I can never thank God enough for *protecting* me because my life definitely could have been worse off. I could have lost my mind, battled depression, went on a sexually driven escapade, the list goes on. If you are reading this, I am believing God will keep you, heal you and help you navigate as you seek to find peace, healing, balance and more in your life.

As I revisited my story, I spent time telling those who are close to me about my sexual abuse experience. For the first time in my life, I shared my story with more than a handful of people. I literally only told five people prior to me telling everyone else. But I knew God was leading me to tell my story. I didn't want them to be blindsided once my story came out. I knew I was releasing part of it, or at least the fact that I was sexually abused, but not in depth of what actually happened on the YouTube channel my wife and I oversee.

As I told others, emotions came up that I didn't know were there. Tears filled my eyes as I told certain people, and I'm not a person who easily cries. As supportive as everyone who I talked to was, I still had thoughts of doubt: "Should I really tell this story?" "Once it's out there, it's out there." I even contemplated deleting my YouTube video before it was posted. As the time kept getting closer for it to post, I became more anxious and found myself watching the clock until it was posted. I never would have even imagined I would have those emotions, feelings and thoughts. But even in my emotions, feelings and thoughts, I shockingly found out that three of the people I told were also sexually abused, molested and/or raped. That really played a pivotal role in the emotions and tears I was experiencing. To find out three people opened up and told me this happened to them as well was life-altering. That's a tough pill to swallow. It's proof that the issue of sexual abuse is a lot more common than it's talked about.

My sexual abuse happened while my family and I were visiting my stepdad's side of the family. We probably visited where he was from about once a year. I've even been there visiting without Ma before, but nothing ever happened before or after. This particular trip, I was sexually abused by an older girl cousin. I remember bits and pieces of the trip down there. I remember the night of the incident. But nothing of the day, other events of our time there after the incident. I don't even remember the drive home after. It's all blacked out. I wish I could remember every detail to give you a more detailed story. I do know we were at a hotel. We had just come back from playing in the swimming pool. My older girl cousin and her older brother were at the hotel with us. Let's call the girl Marissa and let's call her older brother Kent.

We all went back to the room—Ma, Marissa, Kent and me. Marissa and Kent were spending the night with us at the hotel. I remember Marissa, Kent and I were laying on the bed from the pull-out couch. Ma and my stepdad were in the room with the door closed, sleeping. We were just watching TV. I don't know how the conversation came up, but I know she was the one who asked it.

"Do you want to have sex?"

She may have asked it in a different way. Maybe she explained it or maybe she didn't have to. I remember she was laying against me. I remember her brother looking back and asking what we were talking about. She told him in so many words to mind his business and leave us alone. That's the only dialogue I remember him saying the entire night.

I asked her, "Right now?"

Her response was something along the lines of, "No, silly. Not right now. But when my brother goes to sleep."

She laid close to me until Kent fell asleep. I remember Kent falling asleep, but I don't remember the buildup. Did we start kissing? Did she take my clothes off after she took her clothes off? I do remember there being a sink in the living room. I specifically remember being under the sink, fully naked with her on top of me, grinding and kissing me. We were on the side of the pullout mattress with her on top of me kissing me. I only remember those two scenes in my mind. I can't tell you how it ended. I can't tell you how we finished. I can't tell you how we stopped. Maybe Kent woke up and we stopped. I can tell you Ma and my stepdad didn't know or catch her (us) because it would have been a bad scene that night. What I do know is this was the only "incident."

But once is more than enough.

I have forgiven Marissa. I hold no grudge against her. I don't wish her any ill will. I might have seen her one time after that, but I haven't seen her in probably 25+ years. I just wonder what she was exposed to that she knew what to do and how to do it. Someone older than her had to mess with her, as well. Who was the original predator that exposed her to things only adults that are married should know? If it was a predator, who else has this person messed with, hurt, sexually abused or misused? How far back does it go? What is the root and who started it? I'm not justifying what my offender did. I just think about how many people could have been affected. That's what breaks my heart. Thinking about the one whose life was drastically changed and/or cut short as a result of being sexually abused, molested and/or raped. In the case of my offender, I truly believe it was because something happened to her. We didn't grow up in an era of Porn Hub or the internet (Thank God). I truly believe someone planted that seed of perversion in her and she was just doing what she knew and experienced. In my era, someone had to buy their porn on either VHS (or DVD later toward 2000). She had to get it from someone, which makes me even more sad. That's at least one more child affected by sexual abuse.

This experience, mixed with generational curses and iniquities, sent my life in a downward spiral sexually. Mix in being exposed to pornography at an early age and that gave me a false sense of what love and a relationship was. I can also recall a separate scenario when I was a child where a girl a few years younger than me wanted me to "hump." She got on top of me (clothes on, never what I experienced) and we would hump. But what was she exposed to that she even knew how to do that? My experience opened a door for me to later have a masturbation problem from about age eleven until the age of twenty-three. One thing I noticed is that God kept me from some things.

For example, I could have sex with women. But I could never go to the extreme of hit it and quit it. I was too much of a nice guy. I was always respectable. It's the way God designed me. I never wanted to sleep with any and every woman, despite society, my peers, family and friends telling me I should. I spent more time searching for a girlfriend or trying to have a girlfriend than I did pursuing one-night stands. My experience of sexual abuse definitely had pornography be an unknowing vice for me. It had become so common for me to watch it that I watched it like regular movies. One time in my late teens when I was visiting home from college, my Ma walked in on me watching it. I was fully clothed, and I wasn't masturbating (yet). The bad part was I saw her walk into my first room (I had two connecting rooms), and I didn't bother to get up to turn it off.

She walked in and said, "What are you doing, son?"

I said, "Nothing. Watching this movie. I think it's funny. Look at his socks."

I had a serious problem with pornography and didn't realize it. I didn't realize my experience, mixed with an exposure to porn, were directly linked. Because my sexual abuse experience was with an older girl, not an older male, I subconsciously didn't see the problem at the time. My experience definitely affected me consciously, but more subconsciously, which I believe to be even more dangerous.

I didn't know I needed deliverance. I didn't know I needed God's help because society, family and friends told me, "You had sex with an older girl! You actually got to live what most people dream of. In fact, you should be grateful!"

Despite the words of Ma, "Hoy, you let me know if anyone touches you," I interpreted "anyone" as just a male/man.

God has drastically healed me, changed me and delivered me. He has opened my eyes to so many things, revealed so much. I had a false perception of reality and definitely a false sense of how a relationship should be, especially sexually. I spent a great deal of my relationships and sexual encounters trying to be a porn star in the bedroom. I imitated what I had witnessed for years. I can't imagine growing up in this day and age where it is so easily accessible. All you need is a smart device and the internet. I can imagine I would have been even further off the path God called me to.

My false sense of relationship, love, intimacy and sex carried into the beginning of my marriage to my awesome wife, Jasmin Monk. God had to, and is still, teaching me how to effectively and properly love—not just my wife—but every single relationship in my life. You don't realize it, but you can either consciously or subconsciously develop trust issues. It becomes hard to let people get close to you and for you to be vulnerable to others. I became so guarded that I didn't want to be around too many people. As big as I am, now looking back, I can find myself shrinking in many rooms, if I didn't know anyone there. People never took me as an introvert. But I like to say I am an introvert turned extrovert by God.

I wonder if my experience caused me to subconsciously shut out the world and be an introvert. Growing up, I was "good" by myself. I didn't need or desire human interaction (early in my life). I always wanted to be alone. Only a select few could knock on my door without me getting an attitude. It was so easy for me to throw a relationship away over the slightest thing. I could literally be done with someone, family or not, over the littlest thing and not think twice about it. I would be unaffected and unbothered. I'm just now getting to the point over these past seven years where I am okay with being vulnerable to others and trusting others. But that's the dangerousness of dealing with something subconsciously vs. consciously. I never saw the problem. No one else saw the problem (except God). No one knew the root of the problem. So, there was no solution or remedy needed. I didn't realize I needed one.

It wasn't until God started unpacking things and opening my eyes to things that I knew there were issues. I definitely wasn't able to fully love others the way God had instructed us to. Heck, I didn't become fully vulnerable to my wife until about our ninth or tenth year of marriage. I told her: "I feel like I can be fully vulnerable with you. I trust you." All that time before, I was vulnerable, and I trusted her. But subconsciously, I was not doing so fully. Because of what happened to me, coupled with the fact that I was cheated on by my high school girlfriend, I never wanted to feel that pain again. So, I was consciously skeptical of women and even more subconsciously skeptical. Now in defense of my high school girlfriend, I was no saint. I got what I deserved. My little plan was to mess around with other girls until I married her later in life, then stop—extremely dumb thinking. I even had another girlfriend at my high school that knew I had another girlfriend at another high school. So, I definitely wasn't innocent. But as you can see, my experience, mixed with generational curses and iniquities, led me on a downward spiral. But God kept me and that's the beauty of God. He was, and is, willing to show me how to be better, how to become who He sent me here to be. He was patient with me, keeping me and guarding me. I am forever grateful for God!

In essence, I believe that I have only healed, and yet still am healing, with the help and guidance of God. I would love to say that I am fully healed, but I truly don't know because I had so much subconscious pain, hurt, anger and trauma. But I am committed to the journey and process of fully healing. Although I cannot distinctively say I'm fully healed, I can, without a shadow of a doubt, say that I am definitely better than I was when it happened. I am definitely better than I was a year ago and last month. God is taking me from glory to glory. I just have to be willing to want to be better. That's why I want to tell my story. I believe God is leading me to also to help others (especially men) know they have a voice, and they can be healed of their traumas, both consciously and subconsciously.

You don't have to just let someone take advantage of you (especially an older woman or girl). It's not a badge of honor or accomplishment. Your body belongs to you, and you don't have to give in, take it or allow it because society, family or friends tell you it's the cool thing to do. No child, boy or girl, should ever experience these things. We just have to do a better job protecting our children. We must stop protecting the predators or offenders in families. With the help of God, we have to create a safe environment for our children to flourish, in Jesus' name. I especially want to bring awareness to older women/girls taking advantage of young boys and young girls. It happens more often than not. Many boys don't say anything because they don't want to be laughed at or talked about when they are genuinely trying to express their feelings. Who wants to be ridiculed, called names or blown off like they shouldn't be telling these things? Children should feel and be loved. They should feel and be safe.

Protect and love the children because they deserve to be protected and loved. But don't stop there! Properly love adults, as well. Break the chain. Break the pattern. Break the generational curses and iniquities. Realize that children are also the most important part of our future. Give them the best chance to be all God sent them here to be. Help them launch off a higher platform than we did, in Jesus' name.

If you have never heard it, or if you don't hear it enough, know that I believe in you! I love, cherish, value and appreciate you!

Breaking the Cycle of Silence
Reflection Questions

1. Was there ever a time you were made to feel that your emotions didn't matter? How did that make you feel?

   _____

   _____

   _____

   _____

   _____

2. How can you help create a safe space for men to share their emotions?

   _____

   _____

   _____

   _____

   _____

3. How often do you make sure you are in a healthy space mentally?

_____

_____

_____

_____

_____

4. How do you believe this world could become a better place?

_____

_____

_____

_____

_____

5. How often do you tell others you love them and are genuine about it? If not, why not?

_____

_____

_____

_____

_____

ABOUT THE AUTHOR

Hoy Monk II

What many see as helpless and hopeless he sees as whole. For Hoy Monk II, author, director and pastor, his greatest level of success doesn't just come from fulfilling his own purpose and destiny—but his innate ability to usher others into a life of fulfillment. Unlike many people who see the flaws and faults of others first, Hoy has been graced with the heart of God and always sees the best in others. Despite how a situation may look or seem, despite what a person's past says about them, he is quick to see them at the point of redemption—even if they're not there yet.

Ordained as a pastor in 2019, Hoy believes that each individual is unique and that we were all created on purpose, with purpose by God. Hoy is known for believing when things look good—and believing even more when it seems all hope is lost. Set apart as the Youth and Young Adults Pastor at Detroit World Outreach Christian Center, he's on a mission to fulfill the totality of his God-given assignment and draw others to God in the process. As he changes the spiritual trajectory of his immediate family, his life becomes a walking epistle. He models how one can successfully live for God and enjoy life.

His debut book, *An Experience: A Book of Poems*, is a compilation of poetic prose and floetry that tackles some of life's most taboo topics. In addition to completing the audio book, Hoy will also release the stage production in 2020. His debut short film, *Hurt*, will also be released in 2020. Through the written word, this creative genius is on a mission to effect change in the entertainment and media world for the glory of God—advancing the kingdom of God on a global scale. Featured on *Rocki's Reality Radio Show*, Hoy is committed to under promising and overdelivering, no matter what platform he stands on.

In a time and season where many people are worried about "their four and no more," it's enlightening to know someone who genuinely cares about your well-being, your destiny and your God-ordained purpose. Hoy is that someone. He is consistently and intentionally believing and pulling for others to win—offering them grace and redemption at all points of their journey.

For interviews or booking, email itshowyouwordit@gmail.com or visit www.hoymonk.com.

Hardwood Floors
TENITA C. JOHNSON

Untouched

Cold hardwood floors couldn't cover the stench
that's forever ingrained in my nose.

Chilly, freezing almost, I feared asking,
"Can I just put back on my clothes?"

The fact that we had to hide let me know it was wrong—somewhat;

Fear of what my family would say
made me feel like a hoe, a tramp, a slut.

Many days, I lay awake waiting for the pain, the shame to subside,

Only to find myself searching for a deeper place to hide.

Grandma always talked about God, but where in the hell was He?

"Dear God, can you even honor a prayer from a kid like me?"

Married, children of my own; yet, still locking up.

I've grown. I've matured. But I'm mentally, spiritually, stuck.

You can take a poor black girl out the hood;

Make her put on masks and act like life is all good.

But when depression, suicidal thoughts and
bouts of lust become her crutch,

Does the God that she sings about, heard about,
have the power to render her untouched?

>———<< ● >>>———<

I was addicted, and I didn't even know it.

The funny thing is that I didn't even realize my form of addiction until I was well into my marriage, which I was singlehandedly tearing up piece by piece. Unlike the good, wholesome Christian girls, I was sexually active with my husband long before we said, "I do!" Even at the young age of fourteen, I wanted sex. But I was *terrified* every time we started. My legs always seemed to lock up before the initial entrance of his penis into my vagina, almost making it impossible for him to penetrate. It always took a few moments for me to get into the mood and groove of it. But once my mind caught up with our bodies, which were midway into the act, I was able to relax and enjoy the ride. As a teenager, my then boyfriend was patient with me when he basically had to pry my legs open for me to relax and "let him in." However, when we married, and I was still locking my legs to the strength of a horse's legs, my husband knew something was seriously wrong.

And it had nothing to do with *him*. It had everything to do with *me*.

>———<<< ● >>>———<

I had to be seven years old when I had my first sexual experience. Since my mother had birthed me at fourteen, I stayed with my grandmother most times. Although my mother lived in the same house, my childhood memories of her are faint. Of course, she had to finish and graduate high school and work. But, when both my grandmother and my mother weren't available to watch me, my older female cousin watched me. Ironically, I always asked to go spend the night over my cousin's house, but my mother and grandmother often refused. I didn't know why back then, but I've come to terms with their reasoning now.

My grandmother had hardwood floors throughout her tiny courtway building apartment, where my mother and I, and sometimes my drunk uncle, resided. There was only one bedroom in the apartment, which my grandmother let my mother sleep in. My grandmother's bedroom was actually what should have been the dining room. I'm not sure why or whose idea it was, but I slept in the bed with my grandmother nightly. By the time I was three or four, my grandfather had passed. I have no recollection of him. But, by the way my aunts and uncles talk about him, he wasn't a nice man. Piece by piece, I've picked up that he was abusive in more ways than one to my grandmother and his children. No one in the family will give me the specifics, but as I peel back the layers of history untold, I'm left to imagine the agony and pain my grandmother more than likely endured.

While many people remember waxing hardwood floors on their hands and knees, my memories of the hardwood floors are a tad more gruesome. It was where she laid me. Those hardwood floors were where I first experienced oral sex—both giving and receiving. The pain of lying on my back on the floor, and later placing my knees on the floor to return the favor to her, followed me well into adulthood. She didn't necessarily tell me not to tell anyone; it was almost understood.

We always had to do *it* on the *side of the bed* on the floor, instead of on the actual bed.

We always did it when no one else was home.

Many times, we even closed the blinds to make the room darker.

I didn't know it then, but in that exact moment, the root of shame was planted. As a teenager, even though I desired physical sex, I refused oral sex from boys. And I refused to give it to them. I told them I didn't like it. I told them it was nasty and uncomfortable. The truth is that every time someone performed oral sex on me, it reminded me of those *hardwood floors*. So, it was safer for me to simply refuse oral sex from anyone even though, many times, I didn't climax from physical sex.

By the time I was fourteen, not only was I addicted to sex, but I was addicted to masturbation and pornography. I found greater pleasure in pleasing myself than engaging in any sexual act with a boy. I can't pinpoint the exact moment I was introduced to pornography; it was almost like it simply *appeared* in my life—and refused to leave. I was in church, but I didn't have enough conviction to stop having sex, watching porn or touching myself. I told myself that I wasn't harming anyone else, and it wasn't a sin if I was engaging sexually with myself. In those days (sometimes weeks) that I tried to stop having sex, porn and masturbation was my drug of choice. I was trying to medicate something that was so much deeper than any pill or alcohol bottle could fulfill. I was attempting to satisfy the crave of lust. I was attempting to fill the void of not having a father tell me that I was worth the wait. I was rocking myself to sleep spiritually, often masturbating two or three times a day when no one was home, only to fall into a deep sleep.

I told myself that I *needed* it. I need to feel like I'd felt the first time I actually started to *enjoy* the oral sex my cousin performed on me. I needed to feel the release. I needed to feel in control of pleasing myself when no one else around me felt like I was worth it. I equated the sex, the porn, the masturbation to love. The reality is I was chasing what I now know as the spirit of lust, which was masked as *love*.

In college, I found myself sleeping with too many men to count, many of them whose names I can't remember. From one-night stands when we left the club drunk, to "hidden" relationships with college fraternity men—who invited me over once the sun went down but acted like they didn't know me when they saw me at the student center. Even in college, I was against receiving oral sex. I told myself I didn't need it. I could please myself much faster and easier. But with a little alcohol in my sister, I gained enough courage to perform oral sex on men—something I vowed I would never do. By the end of freshman year of college, I had contracted chlamydia—*for the second time.* When my mother found out I was sexually active at fourteen, just as she had been, she took me to the doctor for testing. I tested positive then for chlamydia and brushed it off. Because there is a cure, a series of pills, I didn't take it as serious as AIDS or HIV. I knew I was going to live. So, I continued to live haphazardly in college.

When I later caught up with the man who is now my husband at the age of twenty, he was shocked that I even offered to perform oral sex on him. Again, we'd been sexually active with each other since I was fourteen years old. He wasn't used to the twenty-year-old Tenita. But he didn't refuse, either. Once again, he tried to perform oral sex on me, and I refused. All I could think about was those *hardwood floors*. I told him I simply didn't desire it. I didn't need it. It was as if I had watched so much porn, and pleased myself so much, that no one else could please me sexually. If it didn't look, sound or feel like sex did in porn, it wasn't real to me. It wasn't good enough.

At the time, I didn't know about human trafficking. I didn't know that many of the women in pornography are under the influence of drugs, or they are forced to perform sexual acts in front of the camera against their will—and actually act like they are enjoying themselves! I didn't know that masturbation was a sin. I thought as long as I wasn't hurting another human being, and I wasn't in fornication, that I was living a righteous life. As I matured in Christ, God began to ask me thought-provoking rhetorical questions. He already knew the answers. But He had to ask me in a certain way to get me to see sin the way He sees sin.

He asked me, "Would you masturbate in front of your children or your husband? Would you watch porn if your husband was lying next to you? Why do you think you masturbate multiple times a day, and you can never seem to get enough?"

I hung my head in shame and awe, already knowing the answers to the questions, unfortunately. That's when God revealed to me how to know the difference between light and darkness. There is no in between. He reminded me that, every time I prepared to masturbate, I closed the blinds or drapes to darken the room. When I had sex with men, I always needed to have sex under the covers or sheets. I didn't like a man looking at me naked in the light—or even without the sheets covering my body for that matter. I didn't even like having sex in the morning time. My drive was (and still is) at its highest at night. The truth of the whole matter was that I would never masturbate or watch porn in the room with my children or my husband because of the level of *shame* I'd developed over time. Shame had taken root at the age of seven and refused to let me go. I would stop during fasts or during weeks where I was extremely busy. But as soon as I had idle time, the thought to masturbate or watch porn reared its ugly head once again.

When I married my husband, he said something to me that, at first, offended me. The truth usually does, though.

He said, "You equate sex to love. And if we're not having sex, you feel like I don't love you."

I was ashamed of that truth, but he had hit the nail on the head, allowing it to pierce the very depths of my soul. In that moment, I was confronted with the ugly truth that many attempt to sweep under a rug—leaving them shackled to shame, fear, guilt and low self-esteem. When my husband was angry with me, and we didn't have sex for days or weeks at a time, I thought he was going to leave me. He threatened to leave me many times before, so it was only a matter of time before he actually left and didn't come back. So, I thought. He was going to leave me, just like my mother and grandmother had left me with my older cousin, who introduced me to oral sex. He was going to leave me like my father had left me—destitute and broken without a clear definition of my identity. He was going to leave me, alone and depressed.

To my surprise, no matter how many times he threatened to leave, through every storm, he chose to stay. Even after my infidelity when our marriage was in shambles, he chose to love me through it. He chose to pray me through it. He chose to cover me in prayer and speak well over me. He supported me by paying for six years of individual counseling, which totally transformed my mind and, hence, our marriage. Many people get into a marriage and think that they need years of marital counseling. The truth is most people need some form of individual counseling before they attempt to join in holy matrimony to anyone. I didn't know who I was in Christ when I married. I didn't like myself. I battled suicidal thoughts and bouts of depression too many times to count. And, unlike many people think, my addiction to masturbation and pornography didn't cease when I got married.

If anything, it increased. When my husband was mad at me, or tired from work, I defaulted to pleasing myself. It was quicker and I didn't have to deal with him rejecting me. I didn't know I was building taller invisible walls that he would later have to tear down every time we tried to be intimate. I didn't realize the spirit of division and lust that I was allowing to operate in my marriage. As long as I didn't step outside the marriage with another man, I didn't consider it cheating on my husband. It took the wisdom of one pastor to open my eyes to the damage I was causing unintentionally.

He said to me, "When you masturbate, or watch porn and please yourself, you are operating in a form of prostitution."

I wasn't a prostitute! I'd never worked a street corner a day in my life. The raw truth will first offend you, then it will change you. In the Word of God, 1 Corinthians 6:19-20 (NIV) says, *Do you not know that your bodies are temples of the Holy Spirit, who is in you, whom you have received from God? You are not your own; you were bought at a price. Therefore honor God with your bodies.* Prostitutes don't honor God with their bodies. They use their bodies to earn money, which has become their God. And, I'm sad to say, I was no better than them.

As I matured in my walk with Christ, I realized if I was going to truly break this stronghold, I had to be intentional about my time. I had to be intentional about what I allowed to enter my ear gates and eye gates. I immediately asked my husband to cancel the subscription to premium channels on cable. I threw out all of my pornographic DVDs in large, black trash bags. That's how many I had acquired since college. I started being strategic about what I watch on TV. I can't watch sex scenes, or even some kissing scenes, in a movie or a TV show. I immediately get aroused. I know I can't listen to certain music, either. Although I love Brian McKnight, if I listen to him, I immediately fall into a sensual, sexual mood. There are even certain songs or albums that remind me of old flings from college that I simply know I can't listen to. I also gave certain friends permission to hold me accountable to my healing and deliverance journey. My friends would call or text me and ask if I had watched porn or masturbated recently. They prayed with me over the phone or in person too many times to count. This is a stronghold that requires accountability, prayer, counseling and more to break. Its roots run deep.

I'd be lying if I told you the thoughts don't come anymore. More times than not, those thoughts come when no one is home and I'm sleepy or sluggish. They come when I lie down at night and my husband may not be in bed yet. Of course, if I watch a show or a movie, or listen to a certain type of music, my desires are heightened. But I know firsthand the damage masturbation and porn has caused to me as an individual, a wife and a mother. My husband and I are strategic about making sure these strongholds don't get passed on in our bloodline to our children or their children. We don't want our children to ever experience molestation. We don't want our children to have to work through pulling up the roots of strongholds like masturbation and addiction to pornography. We want our children to live wholesome lives as individuals and spouses once they marry and have children of their own. Life in general has enough trouble on its own. We don't want our children to carry any extra baggage into their next journey of life.

It took me years to learn it, but now I understand that masturbation and addiction to pornography is another form of slavery. Mentally, I was bound and shackled. I needed my "fix" every day, multiple times a day. The enemy wanted to keep me "high" and strung out on drugs that society doesn't know how to rehabilitate. There was no five-step program or detox program that would allow me to go cold turkey. I had to walk out the journey of healing and deliverance day by day, hour by hour, minute by minute, as the Holy Spirit revealed the underlying roots and effects that kept me stuck wanting more. God was patient enough with me to reveal those things I was mature enough to handle as I walked through the journey. He didn't dump it all on me at once. He lovingly slowly, but surely, transformed my mind and allowed me to see those things as He sees them.

Many times, we make excuses for our sin. We say, "God knows my heart." We take God's grace and mercy for granted. We focus on God's love, but not His correction. The Word of God is clear. Whom He loves, he chastises, just as we do our own children. For years, I told myself that I needed to masturbate or watch porn to go to sleep. I needed it to fulfill my lustful desires so I wouldn't have sex with anyone. I needed it to make myself feel good, to make myself feel worthy of love. However, one thing is for certain: light and darkness cannot coexist. As soon as light shows up in a room, darkness ceases. God is that light. When He showed up in my life, and truly began to walk me through total transformation, any sign of darkness had to cease.

I had to forgive my cousin. After all, someone had to be touching her inappropriately in order for her to perform oral sex on me in her youth. Where does a child get that from? It had to be deposited into her in order for her to perform the act. I had to forgive my mother and grandmother for leaving me vulnerable. I had to forgive them for not protecting me enough to not let this happen over and over again. I had to forgive them for keeping so many family secrets that it kept not only them bound, but me as well. I now realize that I'm not just working through my individual strongholds. I'm yet working to uproot those things that were passed on to me from generations of people who chose to suffer in silence. I'm yet working to uproot the family curses that continue to try to ride on the bloodline. My husband and I are strategic and intentional about telling our children what we have been through and overcome—so that they don't have to fight the same battles. We work to heal marriages and families across the nation, allowing them to break generational curses off their family bloodline and rewrite their family history.

There's so much in my life that remains a mystery. I'm certain that as I grow in my relationship with Christ, He will reveal that which I am able to accept and process healthily.

People say, "What you don't know can't hurt you."

I beg to differ. It's those things that *I didn't know* that affected my life the most, unfortunately.

Be committed to your individual healing. The transformation you want to see starts with *you*.

Breaking the Cycle of Silence
Reflection Questions

1. What individual strongholds do you need to work through to get total healing and deliverance?

_____

_____

_____

_____

_____

2. Who do you need to forgive in order for you to be totally free?

_____

_____

_____

_____

_____

3. What happened to you a child that has negatively affected
    your marriage?

    _____

    _____

    _____

    _____

    _____

4. What is God's purpose for your marriage?

    _____

    _____

    _____

    _____

    _____

5. What has God revealed to you about *you* that you need to
    come to grips with?

    _____

    _____

    _____

    _____

    _____

ABOUT THE AUTHOR

Tenita C. Johnson

Transforming pain into purpose is a gift that authorpreneur, speaker and book coach, Tenita "Bestseller" Johnson gives to everyone she encounters. She is a warrior of words with a fierce passion for guiding authors to expand their brand by showing them how to earn multiple streams of income from just ONE book. As the author of 18 books, seven of which have been Amazon bestsellers, she is living proof that sharing your story leads to your destiny.

Familiar with rising from numerous fires and coming out unscathed, Tenita has triumphed over suicidal thoughts, depression, low self-esteem, marital storms and blended family woes. She has also endured miscarriages and the still birth of twins the day after she married her husband. Each of these tragedies has added indelible layers to her resilience. With more than 25 years in journalism, writing and editing, she has a knack for creating narratives that are authentic and raw, yet endearingly relatable. She is a vessel with the ability to change lives and impact the world, thus she is a proud "book bully," who relentlessly urges others to, "Write the book and get paid for the pain!"

When Tenita speaks, people listen with their ears as well as their hearts and souls because her transparency transcends pretense. She is a bold beacon of hope who inspires others to seek their highest peak. One of her proudest and defining moments was her appearance on Kirk Franklin's Praise Sirius XM channel.

As the founder and CEO of So It Is Written Publishing, she has helped hundreds of authors birth their books in record time. The 12-year-old company excels as a one stop shop for the complete book process from conception to completion, not just editing. The editorial guru successfully helps people to pen books that will boost their brand, accelerate their paydays and bust open doors of endless opportunities. So It Is Written won The Sunrise Pinnacle Award for Diversity Company of the Year, in 2020, from the Rochester Regional Chamber of Commerce in Rochester, Michigan. For six years, Tenita hosted the Red Ink Conference in Atlanta, Detroit, Charlotte and Chicago. Over 600 attendees received invaluable information from industry leaders on how to write, edit, market and publish their next bestseller.

Beyond her books, her versatility shines in multiple areas, including her role as the executive producer of the hit stage play, *When the Smoke Clears*, which was based on her book, *When the Smoke Clears: A Phoenix* Rises. The play ran in 2017 and 2018 to sold-out audiences in downtown Detroit. She also served as the editorial director for *Career Mastered Magazine* and *Hope for Women Magazine*. Currently, she is the national president of The Aspiring Writers Association of America, a writers' organization that works with writers worldwide to pen their next literary masterpiece.

Tenita's passion for delivering bestselling books is matched only by her devotion to helping women and men heal from the drama, trauma and baggage of sexual abuse. Her 2021 anthology, *HUSH: Breaking the Cycle of Silence Around Sexual Abuse*, features eight women who lost their innocence and identity to life-altering trauma. She is a huge advocate and mouthpiece for those who have been sexually abused as she empowers them to release their pain instead of suffering in silence.

Her future plans include producing her short film *What Happens in This House* and completing the script for her feature film *When the Smoke Clears*. As a catalyst for positive change, she is a woman who has learned to live an intentional life of purpose while unapologetically fulfilling her God-driven assignments.

For booking or speaking engagements, email info@soitiswritten.net or visit www.tenitajohnson.com.

The Sin of Silence
A Story of Familial Sexual Abuse & Trauma
THEO TUCKER

I was born in the 80s. My mother's family was extremely close. I mean, *The Cosby Show* close. We did everything together. We went to parks, watched sports, had barbecues, enjoyed birthdays. My entire youth was full of family experiences, most of them being centered around my grandmother's house on the west side of Detroit. My grandmother was the epitome of the essence of "Big Momma." She woke up at the crack of dawn, cooking and cleaning. She fed everyone who crossed her path. She loved her six children unconditionally and she loved her ten grandchildren the same way.

I was the second-born grandchild to the family, but I was the first grandson. My older cousin, Daphne, was six years older. You can imagine how excited everyone was when I was born. I was spoiled beyond necessity. I was adored. I was *special*.

As we grew older, and more grandchildren came into the picture, I never stopped being special in my grandmother's and grandfather's eyes. I was allowed to go shopping with my grandmother. I was given permission to walk to the corner store without an adult. I could stay up later. I could skip nap time. I got to be in the kitchen with my grandmother while she was cooking. My younger cousins were jealous, but I enjoyed the exclusivity. Daphne was in middle school by this time, so I was really the only one who got to do these things. I was *special.*

A few years passed, and there was a day at my grandmother's house that forever changed me. It changed my life. I was in the basement with several of my cousins. This was typical. The basement was our space. It's where we ate Thanksgiving dinner as kids. It's where we played with our toys at Christmastime, so we didn't clog up the living room. Most importantly, it's where we were able to spend our time, play, listen to music, and just be kids. The main room of the basement was really my uncle's haven. There was a pool table that we weren't allowed to touch, a bar, and an amazing stereo system, complete with an 8-track player, a record player and two tape decks.

One afternoon, as I was playing with my cousins and my younger brother, we heard footsteps coming downstairs. We were shocked to see Daphne standing in the doorway. The thing is, Daphne *rarely* came downstairs with us. I honestly can't remember five times that she ever played with us down there. I figured she was bored out of her mind and resorted to just hanging out with her younger cousins.

She said, "What y'all doing down here?"

We happily told her that we were making a movie, because we thought we were all destined for Hollywood!

Daphne suggested that we act out a movie we'd never heard of before.

She said, "Let's play 'The Burning Bed'." We were confused because we didn't know what she was talking about. Years later, we realized that we *shouldn't* have known about this movie. So, we asked her what the movie was about. She reassured us that we should just follow her lead and that she would be the main character. We were honestly so pleased that our oldest cousin was playing with us that we blindly followed her lead.

At one point, Daphne said she and I needed to act out the most important scene in the movie. That scene took place in the "bedroom." For us, that meant going into the other side of the basement, where the utility room, washer and dryer, and small bathroom were. So, my other cousins continued playing their parts, while Daphne led me into the utility room. She told me that I had to lay down like I was on the bed, and that she would act out the other part. So, I laid down.

I wasn't nervous until she touched me *down there*. Nobody had ever touched me *there*. I was told to never let anyone touch me there. But surely, this was okay because Daphne was my cousin, my friend, my family. She touched me again, and I asked her what she was doing. I had never felt anything like this before. It felt strange. Not good or bad. Just strange. Daphne told me to be quiet and trust her. That was easy. I *did* trust her. Surely Daphne wouldn't do anything to hurt me. She continued to touch me. Then she put her hand inside my shorts and touched me again. Then came the rubbing. She had her hand around me, rubbing up and down. I didn't understand this at all. I couldn't process what I was feeling. It felt *good*, but it felt *wrong*. I was so confused and started getting really nervous.

What happened next was wrong, even in my naivety. She took my shorts, pulled them down, and then did the same to herself. I was in complete disbelief; I was looking at my cousin, *naked*! She giggled, then proceeded to place herself on top of me. I felt something warm, something tight, an unusual feeling that completely confused me, but also aroused me. Then, she moved. The rocking back and forth was unlike anything I'd ever experienced in my life. She started making noises I'd never heard her make before. And she was breathing heavily. I saw sweat beads form on her forehead. Then, I started to sweat. My breathing became heavy, as well.

I didn't know what to do. All I know is that I wanted her to stop. I asked her to stop. First once, then again. She told me, "Shut up!" Daphne had never talked to me like that before! It didn't feel good. I asked again, and she gave me the same answer. Now I became sad. I didn't like what was happening. I wanted it all to stop. I didn't want to be *special* anymore. I wanted to be left alone. Finally, I got my wish. My aunt, Daphne's mother, called for her to come upstairs. And just like that, the rocking stopped. The breathing normalized. The sweat was wiped away, and shorts were put back on.

"You better not say anything, or I'll beat you down! You hear me?"

Laying there in fear, in confusion, I simply nodded my head affirmatively. As Daphne went back upstairs, I realized I was still laying there naked on the utility room floor. I got up, put my shorts back on, and sat in the small bathroom. I couldn't think, couldn't feel, couldn't breathe. I didn't know how to process what had just happened.

I don't know if it was because I knew it was wrong, or because I felt violated, or because I didn't know what else to do, but the tears started to flow. And they were coming hard and fast. Each tear felt like alcohol on an open wound, further burning the grotesque and despicable violation into my body, mind and soul. What was even worse was that my cries were silent. My brother and cousins were right next door. I didn't want to alarm them to what was going on. My cousins looked up to me. They listened to me. In their eyes, I was still *special*. So, I quickly dried the tears, took a deep breath, and straightened my clothes. I walked out the bathroom and went back into the other room to play with my cousins.

I didn't realize it at the time, but this was a huge turning point in my life. It led me down a very dark path of addiction in four particular areas. *I was addicted to anger.* I need every single man that has suffered sexual abuse to remember this above everything else I share. *An emotionless man is a monster, and he will destroy everything he comes in contact with.*

I learned this principle the hard way. See, in the African American culture, there is a generational toxic principle passed throughout our families, reiterated in society. We teach men that being emotional, or expressing emotion, is somehow feminine and weak. We are taught that any man who does this is not fully masculine. What has happened, as a result, is that men everywhere bottle up their emotions and suppress them constantly. I learned that suppression is a temporary, limited response to the stigma society puts on men. Every container in the world has a limit, including your heart, mind and body. When you overfill a container, the contents either spill out, or the container breaks. The same is true with our emotions. If we keep suppressing them, they will explode and spill out in an uncontrollable way.

That's exactly what happened to me. I was so angry because my cousin, whom I loved dearly, made me feel like I was no longer *special*. She deceived me, she used me, she abused me, for her own selfish desires. Then, she threatened me. She played on my innocence and used my love for her against me. The most hurtful thing was that she got away with it. I wasn't brave enough to expose her. I wasn't strong enough to face isolation from my family. I forecasted a negative conclusion based on my fear and pain. I allowed it to dictate a major chunk of my life. It was a cancer, slowly eating away at me for twenty years.

So, what happened when I got angry? I unleashed hell on whomever or whatever I "thought" I was angry at. See, every little thing was a hair trigger that caused me to detonate. I had no regard for who it was or what the situation was. If you disrespected me, tried to trick me, or take advantage of me, I exploded. Why? Because Daphne got me, and I was never going to allow anyone else to get me again. Nobody else would ever take advantage of me, use me, abuse me, or deceive me. No, I would strike first. And I would strike fast. I was a cobra. I made sure that once I bit you, you weren't coming back. You would never get that close to me.

That's what led to my second addiction. *I was addicted to perimeters*. I enjoyed creating barriers between me and others. My logic was simple: If I kept you at a distance, you would never get close enough to me to deceive me. This was my way of protecting myself. This kept me safe. This prevented me from getting hurt again. The problem is that my trauma was untreated, and this was creating an entirely different barrier that I never realized until much later in life.

Untreated trauma creates a barrier that external love cannot penetrate. There isn't a person walking this earth who can burst the bubble of untreated trauma. It may appear that someone has gotten through it, but it's an illusion. Once the illusion dissipates, the person trying to penetrate this barrier ends up being severely hurt by the one with the trauma. It's like the expression says, "*Hurt people hurt people.*" When you have untreated trauma of a sexual nature, it's almost impossible to truly love anyone, including yourself! There is only one key that opens this barrier. It's only when we have a moment of transparency with God and identify His love for us that the barrier is penetrated.

Only after we acknowledge that, despite what we went through, His love is still perfect toward us, can we begin to heal and experience love from others. Once we can acknowledge His love for us, we can use it as a template to love ourselves, validate our worth, and begin to try to love others. I've learned that the biggest hurdle I had to overcome with this experience was realizing that sexual abuse didn't destroy my value. I still had value. God still valued me. I was still *special* in His eyes!

I also became addicted to a couple of things a lot of sexual abuse victims don't talk about. *I became addicted to my appearance.* This was the most debilitating effect of my trauma. For those who know me currently, this may be hard to visualize. But I was a skinny kid before this happened. After I was abused, I unknowingly made sure that I looked completely different from the version of me that was the object of my violator.

This is more common than most people realize with victims of abuse. Food became the object of my affection, my comfort, my safe place. The more I ate, the more my body changed. The more my body changed, the less I looked like that ten-year-old skinny kid who was abused. The less I looked like my victimized self, the more comfortable I became. I didn't want to keep looking in the mirror and seeing the victim. I wanted to see someone different. And that's a victim mentality. We take extreme measures sometimes to alter what was attractive to our violators. Then we start looking for anyone who will "love" the altered version of us. And that's who we commit to.

Meanwhile, we're building a relationship, a life, on something that's not authentic. We're building a new life based on a lie. We do it because we're tired of seeing ourselves as the person who was raped, violated, taken advantage of. We do it for our own sanity, especially men. I am constantly being told that I can't be emotional, that I'm a punk, and that I'm an outcast from my family if I speak the truth. I am expected—yes *expected*—to continue to be around the source of my trauma as if nothing happened. So, the only outlet I can think of is to make sure that I'm no longer desired by that monster. If I have to make myself unhealthy, so be it!

Lastly, *I was addicted to justice*. I became the defender of everything and everyone around me. I was vigilant everywhere I went. I fought for the little guy. I bullied the bullies. I never backed down from anyone or anything. I channeled my anger into fights, cussing and violence. I feared no one and nothing. I wanted to be the hero who never showed up for me. I wanted to save someone else from feeling the way I felt every day: alone and misunderstood. I didn't want the Daphnes of the world to win again. I wanted the would-be victims to feel *special*.

This especially manifested verbally. I never lost a debate, and I never backed down in a discussion. I would never be silent again. I would never pass up another opportunity to speak up and express how I felt about something. I would never shut up and keep anything to myself ever again! I did it once and look what happened to me! So, I became notorious, a menace to society, a stereotypical angry, young Black man.

This followed me into adulthood, along with depression, pornography and alcoholism, just to name a few. By the time I was set to graduate high school, I was drinking Hennessey like it was apple juice and watching porn religiously. I knew how to suppress it and when to suppress it. At the same time, I was barreling down this deadly road. I was leading worship, participating as a youth leader, and singing in the church choir. Nobody suspected because they were getting what they wanted from me. I was allowing them to use me because they made me feel special again.

Well, the suppression container finally reached its limit. On January 31, 1999, I sat down in the nursery of my church as we were prepping the building for the men's Super Bowl fellowship. I took my switch blade and began cutting my wrists. I was done. I had nothing else to live for. My suppression container broke, and all of my trauma spilled out uncontrollably. I was not going to live another day with this darkness.

God had a different plan.

One of my best friends, Demetria, who wasn't even supposed to still be at church, called out for me as the blade met my skin. She had no idea I was back there or what I was about to do. She said my dad was looking for me. She looked down, saw the blade that I made a poor attempt at trying to hide, and simply asked if I would walk to the playground with her. We talked about high school, college, dreams. We talked for hours. When the sun started to set, she simply gave me a hug and said, "I love you brother. You have more to do."

For the first time since I'd sat in that bathroom at ten years old, I sobbed uncontrollably in her arms. I sobbed tears for every moment that I regretted my experience. I cried for what seemed an eternity, a tear for every moment of suffering and hardship. And, for the first time, I felt love. Not from Demetria, but from God. He loved me enough to send my friend to keep me from killing myself. Even as damaged as I was, He still loved me. That was worth living for. That was worth fighting for. I was *loved*.

Over the next few years, I began the process of healing. I had to fight through the process of forgiveness. I understand that forgiveness is not for the person who harmed you or wronged you, but victims don't really want to hear that. We often don't care about forgiveness; it's justice we're after. For me, I had to realize that the reason forgiveness was for me is because *forgiveness was the key to unlocking my freedom*. And as I forgave, I began to experience freedom.

But the story isn't that clear cut. See, you may begin to experience freedom, but trauma has long-lasting effects. They don't go away suddenly. Trauma must be fought, and you will go some rounds before you can be declared the winner. As free as I thought I was, I didn't realize how much trauma I still had in me until I married. My wife Melissa is everything I could've ever dreamed of in a wife! Sexy, intelligent, saved, funny, sweet, creative, the list goes on! However, none of that stopped me from lashing out at her multiple times. During conversations, she would often tell me that I would cut her off mid-sentence and that sometimes my tone was harsh.

But the most revealing critique she gave me was about my facial expressions. One random day, we were having a conversation. I was expressing my feelings about what we were discussing. I noticed that Melissa took a defensive posture, with a look of fear on her face. I instantly became confused and asked her why she was doing that. She sighed heavily, and said this to me, rocking my world.

"I almost don't want to tell you because you always think that I'm exaggerating and being extra. But I want you to please just listen to me. The look on your face when you were just talking a moment ago was a look of pure disgust. Like I disgusted you. Like I was nothing to you. You looked at me like I was lower than dirt. I've never seen you look at me like that. It seriously made me wonder what I said or did to upset you that much to where you would look at me that way. And look, even now as I'm talking to you, the way you're looking at me is like you could just go off at any moment!"

It was as she said this last part that I realized that my face was completely scrunched up in an aggressive manner. I apologized to her profusely and she forgave me, but it changed our relationship. She now saw that there was an anger inside me that she'd never experienced before. It flashed again after we adopted our daughter Langston. When she's not being obedient, there have been times that I have raised my voice. To a four-year-old, that can be devastating. I never want my daughter to have recollection of her father being verbally abusive. That can set a detrimental precedent for the rest of her life, and I cannot allow that to happen.

So, you see, even though I have forgiven Daphne, I'm still not completely free. Forgiveness is the beginning, not the only thing. Freedom must be fought for, and you will go some rounds before you win your freedom. You may have won the round of life that you're currently in, but more is coming. As life changes, the fight changes. There will come a time soon when I will do my part to teach my daughter about sexual things. I will have to ensure that I don't teach her my trauma, but instead I teach her with the wisdom I have gained from my trauma. This way, she learns what she needs, and I don't pass my trauma along to her. She will get a full chance to experience things for herself.

This experience changed my life forever. It will always be a part of my life, even as a backstory to who I am and what I've gone through. If you are suffering from sexual abuse, please know that it will always be a part of you, but it doesn't have to consume you. It doesn't have to be the thing that controls your life. You can fight. You can forgive. You can be free! I encourage you to learn from my story. I pray that it helps other men gain the courage to speak up and speak out.

It's okay to share.

You are no less of a man for telling your story.

Breaking the Cycle of Silence

Reflection Questions

If you are a man that has suffered sexual abuse, or you are suffering now in silence, ask yourself these questions:

1. Which is more important to protect: your secret or your well-being? Why?

_____

_____

_____

_____

_____

2. What addictions have you inherited because of your trauma?

_____

_____

_____

_____

_____

3. What repercussions, real or assumed, are you weighing
    against your silence?

    _____

    _____

    _____

    _____

    _____

If the abuse hasn't stopped, please tell somebody.
You are too valuable to let this continue.

ABOUT THE AUTHOR

Theo Tucker

The words we speak can be used in powerful ways, and Theo Tucker has dedicated himself to maximizing that power. Known as a wordsmith and inspirational speaker, Theo has worked in various aspects of the literary world, including as an editor with Manifold Grace Publishing, as a ghostwriter for various authors, and as an author himself. Theo has penned multiple books and articles, written manuscripts and even developed curriculums for other authors and motivational speakers. He has also used his words to speak for churches, organizations, companies, to moderate town halls, and as a guest star on various podcasts. Theo's goal is to, "Empower people to create their own lanes of thought and principle through their words, so it's clear to everyone who they are and what they stand for."

Shamed & Silenced
LaTosha A. Lymon

Freedom doesn't just happen. Today, as I sat in solitude, I realized that if I wanted freedom, I mean *true freedom*, from the weight of the trauma that occurred in my life, I had to make an intentional effort to choose it. I opened the door widely to a new level of freedom in finally saying, "Yes" to write and speak about the secret things that happened to me. I wanted to share my experiences simply because it was time. I had never before this time considered writing my story because I believe I minimized what occurred as not being "as bad as" what others I've met have gone through. It is so interesting how life works.

As a Licensed Professional Counselor, I have encountered so many others who had *a story*. As I created a safe, trusting space for them to tell their story, I began to see a reflection of myself in them with each story entrusted to me. I had heard far more gruesome accounts of sexual abuse and molestation. Acts that the heart would not dare to conceive and the mind could not bear to recall, for some. Every time, every story, a part of me cringed and collapsed under the long-existing shame I held, and my inability to do for myself what I had more recently dared others to do in courage- "*write your story.*"

I spent time talking to God about this as I often do about many things, because I am a spiritual person. I asked intently about the significance of me speaking now about what happened to me in the past. Unexpectedly, my mind suddenly focused on the reputation of both of the deceased men responsible for the trauma I succumbed to. I thought to myself, "*I can't bring myself to say things that would ruin other's thoughts of them.*" And as quickly as this thought came to me, it was followed by a small voice within me that spoke up and whispered, "*But what about me?*"

I paused and pondered how so many aspects of my life had been altered by molestation. My understanding was tainted. My heart lost the ability to trust fairly early in life. I became disconnected from my true self. In my mind, my reality shifted from what I believed to what I knew. My eyes were opened in a way that I was not ready for. What I knew and what I witnessed was far too much for my immature, under-developed mind. Somewhere between the ages of eleven and thirteen, my first experience of molestation occurred by a trusted relative who I only saw once a year.

He was a member of my maternal family. I was quite fond of him and had previously held him in high regard. I recall playing outdoors with my cousins on a hot summer day in the south where my family visited each summer. One of my cousins said she wanted to go in the house to get something cold to drink. For some reason, I wasn't going to go in. However, I went against that thought and went into the house.

Most of the lights seemed to be out and it was somewhat dim inside the house because the curtains were closed. We ventured to the kitchen and there I stood near the doorway, waiting for my cousin to do exactly what she came inside the house to do- quench her thirst with a cool drink. I wondered where her father was, but I did not ask. I pushed that thought out of my mind. It wasn't important because we would be in and out quickly. Out of nowhere, he came behind me quietly. He touched me in a place on my body that was forbidden to be touched by a relative. His presence and his touch startled, scared and confused me tremendously. For that moment, I stopped breathing and time stood still. From that moment forward, something inside of me began to shrink. I felt small and insignificant.

My mind was flooded with thoughts, emotions and everything in between. *How could he touch me so freely? Who gave him the right? Didn't he know that I would not be able to handle that? Did he even care?* For the remainder of that visit with my family, every room he walked into, I quietly disappeared from. I adapted quickly, diverting my eyes away from his gaze and, seemingly, devilish grin. While he moved about as freely as he pleased, without guilt, visiting, laughing and talking with other family members, I became more nervous and ashamed. For so many years after that moment, I was ashamed of what happened to me. I thought to myself, *"You should never have gone into that house."*

I pondered sharing with my mother, whom I trusted. But then, my next thoughts became centered around mentally surviving and staying away from that relative for the rest of the time we were there. It was a juggling act each day to avoid his presence. I was so afraid that maybe I was now targeted for something else to happen if I ever found myself alone in any room with him. The mental anguish I forced myself to endure by carrying this secret alone was torture. I couldn't wait for this visit to end and for us to go as far away from there as we could and return home.

Reflecting on this story helped me realize it was most likely the reason I only returned there once, thereafter, to visit and never again. I just could not let my guard down around him. I carried this secret for approximately thirteen years. And, only after he passed away did I finally share it with my mother. My mother wished I had said something sooner. As odd as this may seem, I shared with my mother that my rationale for not sharing it with her sooner was because I did not want to be the reason why she and this relative disconnected. I guess I believed in some way that their bond was more significant than what happened to me.

My second experience with molestation occurred when I was just fourteen years old by a paternal male relative. By this time, I think the other occurrence was buried so deeply in my mind that I had not given it much thought, unless I was asked if I wanted to travel down south to visit family. At fourteen, I thought I was mature enough to have a real boyfriend. I subsequently became sexually active with my boyfriend as our relationship progressed. When I was younger, I was such a compliant child. When my teen years came along, with hormonal changes, my body began to develop a bit more. I was getting an increased amount of male attention and even older adult male attention. This always frightened me, and even more so after this second occurrence.

One day, I asked a favor of my male relative, who I was very fond of. He was always so cool and laid back. He would openly share about life with us all. I always felt comfortable around him until the day that all changed. I asked if he would drop me off at my boyfriend's house this particular day. From time to time, he would drink and casually offered up alcoholic beverages with no penalty if we wanted to try them. This was one of those days. He allowed me to consume a significant amount of beer.

Before long, I was having a new experience and began feeling the effects of the alcohol. He proceeded to take me to my destination. I was so dazed and intoxicated from the beer that I was awake, but not fully aware. Unbeknownst to me, this moment became a prime opportunity for my relative to take advantage of me. With his left hand, he steered the car. With his right hand, he proceeded to touch areas on my body that were not to ever be touched by a relative. Something went off in my brain that something wrong was happening. It felt like I immediately became coherent and alert. Initially, I pushed his hand away, but he pushed back more firmly to proceed with touching me. I pushed him away with more strength in an effort to overpower him and I said, "No! What are you doing?"

This got his attention. Suddenly, this echoing silence came over me. All I could hear outside of the silence was the sound of the radio, but I can't remember what was playing. Back came the confusion, questions and disbelief. I thought to myself, *I must have some type of a target on me. How could this be happening again? What did I do wrong? Didn't he know I trusted him? Did it even matter to him?* Shortly after he pulled up to my boyfriend's house, I got out of the car quietly and didn't look back. All over again, I began to shrink with shame. In the aftermath of it all, I felt like I didn't have a voice. Every other time I encountered this relative, I tried to keep myself out of his view. I tried not to be seen. I wanted in some ways to be invisible. I didn't want to be looked at in a sexual way, especially by individuals who I felt should not see me that way at all.

In the years to follow, I incorporated the popular style of wearing more baggy clothing. Nothing was form-fitting, and I did not wear anything that highlighted my size or shape. I thought this was a measure of protection from the gaze of older men and even from that male relative, whom I saw frequently. I never said a word about what happened. There I was again, keeping yet another secret. There I was again, being my own protector and trying my best to guard myself against what seemed to be lurking predators. This story was revealed to my parents many years later after the individual passed away. My mother was hurt, and my father was angry. I understood why, but I gave my dad the same rationale that I didn't want to be the reason the relationship between him and that relative ended. Over nineteen years later, just prior to his passing, a moment came that was almost perfect to meet alone and share with my relative that I had forgiven him for what happened.

I went to visit him alone in the hospital to check on his wellbeing when I was notified by another family member that he was hospitalized for some routine testing. It alarmed me because he was not usually known for being in the hospital at all. When I heard the news, I felt I had to do this to free him and to free myself, if at all possible. I had a moment when I considered his soul. I thought I would build up the courage to do it. I was so anxious when I walked into that hospital room. He was happy to see me. I was glad to see him being his usual laid-back self, but I was terrified to be alone with him. I had rehearsed what I would say. When I was sitting there, my mind was flooded with so many thoughts.

I thought to myself, "*I can't do this.*" My heart was beating fast, and I was so close to saying something. But it felt like I had a lump in my throat. I went to the bathroom to try my best to calm myself. But each time I came out calm, my heart would start beating fast all over again. In the end, I gave up and walked away. One of the looming thoughts I had was, "*What if he doesn't remember?*" I was not prepared to handle his response if he denied his actions or said he didn't recall what occurred. I cowered in that moment and left the hospital. That night, I went home and wrote down everything I could not say, but wanted to say, to him in that hospital. I said a prayer and I expressed my forgiveness of him in the prayer. I subsequently forgave my other male relative, too.

From time to time after this second relative died, they both crossed my mind. The moments of molestation crossed my mind. I asked God, "*Why did they choose me?*" I wanted to have a moment to talk to them and ask them personally.

I knew realistically that it was a time that would never come, but I still longed for those answers. I wondered if they thought of me and wondered how I was doing in the aftermath of those two moments. I still thought about the things I wanted to say to them. I really just wanted them to hear my voice speak about what happened to me. In my mind, I thought I would share something like this:

"I just wanted to tell you that, after all this time, I turned out to be okay. But that didn't come easily. I imagine you never wondered in that way about me, but maybe you should have. Maybe you should have thought to venture beyond your pain to check in with me, to pray for me, to have positive thoughts on my behalf. I know I can't expect you to do what I would have done in such a situation. Did you know that after that day, after that moment, I started making grown-up decisions that were unhealthy at their core? I began protecting myself before I really knew what it really meant from other older men who looked at me as if I was marked. I loathed the idea of older men and being around them. I became overly cautious. I hated when men would look at me with suggestive eyes and thoughts, seemingly not caring if I was underage. They undressed my teenage body in their minds, forgetting that my body was attached to that of a child... an inexperienced child. Did you know that in my self-protection, and my silence, I protected you while betraying me? I protected and prioritized what I thought to be sacred-family.

All my life, I was good. Ask my parents. They'll tell you. I was the poster child and example for being a "good kid." I didn't do much wrong until after those encounters. I was quiet and sensitive. Then those "moments" came and shattered that persona. I was no longer innocent. My innocence was lost completely against my will and without my permission. So, while I hold you responsible for your actions, I am now able to forgive and release you even more for what happened and free myself so that I can receive a greater level of healing from that part of my past. All that is behind me now because, more than anything, I had to realize that what I needed most was to turn my focus toward freedom. I have let go of the silence and shame associated with being a victim. Now I am reclaiming my "voice"!

Breaking the Cycle of Silence

Reflection Questions

1. In what ways have molestation/sexual abuse changed you?

_____

_____

_____

_____

_____

2. If given a chance, what would you say to the person(s) responsible for your molestation/sexual abuse?

_____

_____

_____

_____

_____

3. Letting go of the shame is a significant step towards freeing
    yourself. In what ways have you made steps toward securing
    your freedom?

    _____

    _____

    _____

    _____

    _____

4. What words would you speak to your younger self after the
    molestation/sexual abuse?

    _____

    _____

    _____

    _____

    _____

5. Many times the abuser has once been a victim. What, in your opinion, is the best way to address a person who is responsible for molestation/sexual abuse?

_____

_____

_____

_____

_____

ABOUT THE AUTHOR

LaTosha A. Lymon

LaTosha A. Lymon is a wounded healer with a story that speaks of one who has overcome and persevered. She is a guide to those who are willing to take the journey toward healing and wholeness as they evolve into being the best version of themselves! LaTosha is passionate about creating a safe, trusting space to help individuals become unstuck and move forward into living a life of freedom and fulfillment. She founded Legacy Life Counseling & Consulting Services, PLLC located in Southfield, Michigan. LaTosha obtained her master's degree in counseling at Ashland Theological Seminary and is a fully licensed therapist in Michigan. She is thoughtfully known as Tosh the LPC!

In private practice, LaTosha serves individuals of all ages with a focus on those who are challenged with anxiety, depression and experiences of unresolved childhood trauma, facilitating individual, group and family therapy work.

Follow LaTosha on Facebook at Legacy Life Counseling & Consulting Services, PLLC and for additional therapeutic resources on Instagram at @ToshtheLPC. For scheduling and booking, please contact her at legacylifeccservices@gmail.com or call 248.234.8576.

———————————————

A Journey to
Self-Awareness & Acceptance
TRACEY BOOKER

I was born in the early sixties in Wilmington, Delaware. I am the elder of two children and the oldest grandchild born to both my maternal and paternal grandparents. As such, much love and adoration were bountifully showered upon me.

I never really wanted for anything. We were an average family, and I grew up with nice things. My parents always made sure that my brother and I were dressed nicely, that we spoke well, and that we always practiced good manners and respected others. My mother and maternal grandmother insisted on my brother and me speaking properly.

Growing up in the sixties and seventies was wonderful to me. It was the time of the quickening pulse and heartbeat of The Civil Rights Movement, Motown, hippies and love children. I remember the assassinations of President Kennedy, Dr. Martin Luther King, Jr., and Senator Robert Kennedy, race riots, and The Vietnam War. I was a happy-go-lucky, deep chocolate brown little girl with a lot to laugh about. I loved going to church, and I didn't have a care in the world, unless I couldn't go to the corner store for penny candy, bubble gum, freeze pops and a nickel bag of *Bon Ton* potato chips. Life was great for this little colored girl. I became "Black" in 1968 when James Brown proudly affirmed for us who we were without shame. I was learning to, "Say it loud!"

There are times when I look at childhood pictures of me and marvel at what I looked like at that time, my hair in particular. I wore ponytails and a bang, but Mom had it in control. I was a typical-looking little girl and what would be considered a "regular size."

My playtime was spent standing at the fence in my yard talking to the neighborhood children. I was not allowed to venture too far away from my mother, who was always somewhere nearby paying attention to what I was doing. I had two groups of neighborhood friends who lived on my street and in back of my house. It wasn't until I was maybe five years old that I was allowed to venture outside of the yard alone. Even then, I also had boundaries as to how far I could go. I didn't play with older children on my street. As a matter of fact, I don't really remember there being many older children in that area. The older children lived near my grandparents.

Around the corner and two short blocks away lived my other "group of friends." They were manifold and diverse in culture and in age. In my neighborhood lived Blacks,

Caucasians, mixed cultures, and other races, but it was predominantly Black. I learned to exist and to play with various children without reference to race until I was about five years old, when I could finally venture out a little. It was with these children that I learned things that were not so innocent. I also learned that race, and our differences as people, really did matter. I learned not to tell my mother everything I learned with these other children, particularly the older ones. Some of these children knew far too much for their age. These children knew how to cuss, but I knew I'd better not do it because I would get a good whipping. Believe me, I didn't want that.

It was some time at this point in my life that I came to hear about sex. The extent of this was that my friends used the "P" word, and they were not referring to a kitty cat. It was a bad word, but some of them heard the word used freely in their homes among their older siblings. Some of these children feigned knowledge of the word and knew the movement of the act, along with how it was related to the anatomy of a woman—all, of course, from a child's point of view or perception. Acting grown up, the older children would share this knowledge with us little kids. Therefore, I came to know the word "p*ssy". The older I got, the more I came to know that if the boys knew this word, they were going to ask you for some of yours. Boys like that became the nasty boys to us good girls. But I was frightened, because it was clear that this was a bad thing to be *talking* about, let alone *doing*. I knew that if my mother found out that I knew, I was going to be in trouble. It was our little secret in the neighborhood. I didn't know specifics; it was a grown-up word that I associated with grown folks. Otherwise, why would it be so hush-hush, such a big secret? The bigger issue was that it was a "bad thing" to do, so I better not be doing it.

By the start of first grade, this thing was monumental. On the first day of school, a little boy in the second grade came up behind me on my ride home on the bus. He announced to the bus and his friends that he liked someone, and he pulled my ponytail and ran away, letting me know that he liked me. He was so cute, but he was also one of the nasty boys. He eventually asked me to give him some of the "p". He knew that word! I was mortified! I was scared, and he kept telling me that I was going to give him some. Oh, my God! I cried, *but I didn't tell my parents*. I was afraid. Sadly, this happens too often, and it happened to me.

The silence.

I was afraid to say anything. Too many girls are molested and raped and never tell anyone.

I want you to understand that silence isn't always golden. The number of individuals who are sexually harassed and/or assaulted has reached epic proportions globally. Fear grips us, and we allow the enemy, in any form, to silence us, thereby having power over us in all of our inherent good. In my ministry and counseling, the number of women and girls I have encountered who have fallen prey to this is heartbreaking. Females who have been sexually abused, molested and raped too often have kept their mouths closed and have become overwhelmed with bondage that hinders their happiness and joy. They are missing the full lives that they are entitled to experience and live as the daughters of God. That is not the way God intends for us to live our lives in Him.

Let me also say this: My parents were not tyrants. But as children sometimes do, they do not share all of what they need to share with their parents for fear that they may get in trouble or that they may have done something to elicit the unwanted behavior, which was my case. This is part of the enemy's ploy to destroy God's anointed ones and to destroy families. The spiritual attack and warfare concerning sex is age old.

In my counseling with females, particularly young girls under the age of eighteen, I find this same pattern of not telling the authority figures—parents, guardians, teachers, pastor—when these things are happening to them. It is disheartening because, so many times, just as in my case, the parent is going to protect the child. But the negative force of fear and bondage has infiltrated their minds and has affected their lives in some way. I learned to be secretive, and it caused me so much pain as I matured. I really had to trust my parents with my life. Imagine that. I could trust them to provide a home, clothes, food and everything else, but a stronghold had me bound at six years old.

Even in all of that, God had me covered. He watched over me and protected me. My parents' prayers covered and undergirded me when I had no idea of what the power of prayer really was. I want you to understand the power of prayer and supplication, as well as the importance of communication with those people who love you. Keeping even the smallest of damaging things to yourself will only cause unnecessary pain, fear and bondage.

I was being sexually harassed at six years old, and I had no idea the battle was just beginning in my young life or that the implications had long-lasting effects.

Somebody Touched Me

The year I started second grade was pivotal. I was seven years old. I was beginning to put on a little weight and becoming chubby; not fat, but I was solid, thick and growing tall. I was the tallest child in my second-grade class. Big-boned folks are on both sides of my family, so there was very little chance that I would ever be skinny.

One Tuesday night, I was in one of the safest places that I could be: my grandparent's house. Because my mom was at night school, working on her bachelor's degree, and Dad was at work providing for his family, it was business as usual for me to be at my home away from home. Grand mommy had come home from work and cooked dinner. Again, nothing up to this point was out of the ordinary.

After dinner, I went to my cousin's bedroom to lie down, and I fell asleep. Out of the stillness of that peaceful sleep, I felt pressure in my vaginal area. It was invasive and unfamiliar, but for some reason I could not open my eyes to see what was happening to me. It was a hand, a large hand, touching and stroking me below my waist. I began to whimper and squirm, but I heard a voice that I will never forget. That voice was one of my cousins who told the molester, *Dude, don't do that to her, man.* The molester laughed. He had a very distinctive laugh. He stopped what he was doing, and they both left the room. Something in me snapped at that moment. I woke up and had the immediate feeling that I'd done something wrong. I was frightened beyond belief and was shaking. I had just been sexually violated by my own cousin. I was in utter shock.

I got out of the bed, went into the hall, and stood by the linen closet door. The bedroom I'd just left was lit, but the hall was dark. And there I was, a frightened little girl standing in the dark, looking into the light, at my grandmother's back. I think that metaphor is significant; standing in darkness, looking toward the light, which showed me protection and love. Just beyond the hall was the living room where my grandmother and other adults were watching television. I was paralyzed with fear and couldn't talk. My mouth seemed to be fastened shut. I just stood there, not making any noise. My grandmother must have felt my presence because she turned around and saw me standing there.

She asked me, "*What are you doing out of bed?*"

I very fearfully told her, "*He* was bothering me."

He quickly spoke up and said that he was just trying to turn me around because I was about to fall out of the bed. This was not true. I was lying flat on my back when he invaded my privacy, and I was nowhere near the edge of the bed. Yet, I never said a word out of fear and his brother never spoke up. My grandmother told me to go get in her bed, which is what I did. But from the very moment of that invasion of privacy, that demonic offense, I was never the same. Memories of what my playmates said about the forbidden word came flooding back.

Molestation, sexual assault, or sexual violence have deep, penetrating roots, implications, ramifications and a history that spans generations. The impact of the various forms of these crimes have deep, piercing effects and how the behavior affects individuals is unique to their experience. The statistics that are reported of the growing number of individuals who have been sexually violated—female and male—grow annually. The proper term for what I experienced at seven years of age is Childhood Sexual Abuse/Assault (CSA), and it is a crime.

The classifications of CSA are manifold. Whether the classification is legal, academic or situational, each categorization may have a different condition on the depth and meaning of the crime. In the most basic classification, CSA is defined as the exploitation of a child, and in this case, that is anyone under the age of sixteen, for the sexual gratification of an adult. Anyone who is sexually abused by another person who is sexually mature and involves the child in any activity that the other person expects to lead to sexual arousal, is committing, or has, committed sexual assault.

When sexual abuse, or sexual assault, is forced upon a child, the vast number of issues that occur as a result of one incident or many repeated acts most likely will have a negative effect on the victim and may be long lasting. The adult perpetrator may be someone who the child knows and has trusted outside of the family. The perpetrator may be a member of the family, a parent, sibling or other family member—which is incest. The child also may experience a same- sex assault, much the same as an opposite-sex assault. Childhood sexual abuse has no boundaries or limitations as to what group of people experience it.

It is important to share that as I began to deal with the effects of the molestation, as a young adult woman in ministry, I was still feeling stigmatized, alone and lonely, as if there was no one who was able to handle pertinent issues such as this within my church. I wanted to be healed and delivered when I began to come out of that twenty-five-year stupor that had me bound in several ways. As I minister on this topic and that phase of my life, I speak in terms of the victimization and how the act leaves innocent and vulnerable people humiliated and fighting for their lives from issues such as post-traumatic stress disorder, depression, anxiety, emotional eating, eating disorders, alcoholism, drug addiction, sexual promiscuity and asexual (lacking interest in or desire for sex) and other behavioral, mental and sexual disorders. Many also experience substance abuse. Spiritual bondage manifests in the lives of the victims.

I could have been affected by many of those negative effects as a result of the molestation. But the main hindrance manifested through emotional eating, my own self-conceptualization, and caring what people thought about me. It took me some time to become delivered from that bondage. I thank God for freedom and liberation in Christ.

Emotional Eating and Weight Gain

As I got older, my life changed not only physically, but also psychologically as a result of the molestation. I ate like crazy! You name it, cake, pie, ice cream, sandwiches, potato chips, candy, breakfast, lunch, dinner, snacks, YUM! I ate and ate. I packed on the pounds. My mother didn't know why I was eating so much. My doctor attributed my weight gain to heredity. They just thought it was a phase. My parents didn't know about the molestation. So, as a result of that fear, I hid the problem with food. Food became my comfort. It really made me feel good. And I didn't have a care in the world about it because I didn't really understand the correlation between my pain and fear and food. I just wanted to keep it coming to bury my frustration and...*my shame.*

By now, I was in the third grade. Like many of my peers, I can remember wanting to do well and get good grades. I was a high achiever. I have vivid memories of third grade and my teacher, in particular. I wanted to be in the top reading group. But no little Black girl, or any girl for that matter, would be in that group in that particular teacher's classroom, circa 1969 – 1970. It was during this year that my weight ballooned. I was tall, solid and thick. Because of my size, I was teased unmercifully. I was bullied. I was intimidated. My life became a giant vat of suffering, in silence, at now eight years old.

But gym class was the one class I enjoyed. It was fun until it was time to be weighed. I'll never forget the day that we went to gym and there stood the school nurse, in all of her glory, with the weight scale. She had the class roll. Being that my last name started with B, my name was first on the list. Innocently, I went to the scale to be weighed. "One hundred pounds!" she announced.

It seemed as if she screamed those words to the rafters so that the entire school could hear, like on the school intercom system! The children in the class thought it was hilarious, and neither the nurse nor the teacher made them stop laughing at me. It was, and still is, one of the most embarrassing moments in my life. If I weren't a dark-skinned child, I would have been bright red. I was the tallest and biggest child in the class, which was another layer in my life to make me feel ashamed. I was already the tallest child in the class, and now this. I had grown by leaps and bounds, standing almost five feet tall.

To add insult to injury, I was also wearing a training bra when I entered third grade. My face looked like a little girl, but certain parts of me didn't. I didn't like the attention I was getting from older boys. I didn't like the fact that I was growing so fast, but I didn't stop eating and I didn't heal. I was addicted to food. I weighed 172 solid pounds in the sixth grade. When I entered seventh grade, I weighed 205 pounds.

The pediatrician put me on a diet and eating plan, but I didn't lose the weight. I continued to gain weight. I began to retreat further into myself and the weight, in addition to the sexual trauma, was affecting me in major ways.

The Battle Continued

As I continued to mature during my pre-teen years, one thing I never seemed to do was to be fearful of grown men—that is, until I reached age twelve. Everywhere I seemed to go, innocently, teenage boys and men thought I was older than I was based upon the shape of my body. I was busty and had a shape that I was always trying to cover up. What I now realize about myself at that time in my life, and have realized with my female clients, is that I didn't want any boys or men to look at me because they looked directly at my breasts.

But the year I was twelve was full of turmoil. I was molested a second time, in public, by a barber.

On some Saturdays, I went to the barbershop with my father and my brother. Of course, it was full of men, but it didn't matter to me. I would either watch television while they all talked or read the *Jet* and *Ebony* magazines that were plentiful there.

This one particular Saturday, the shop was full, and all of the barber chairs were full. The barber who we usually went to was busy, but one of the popular barbers had an opening. My family knew this man, and he had a reputation as being one of the best in the city. So, I went to his chair to have my afro shaped up. While sitting there, he draped my neck and began to cut my hair. My hands were on the arms of the chair. He casually leaned in and placed his penis on my left hand! My God! Because I still had hope in mankind, on one hand, I thought, *Surely, he made a mistake . . . yes, an innocent mistake.* But, on the other hand, I was thinking, *What in the world?* I moved my hand. But again, startled, I didn't say anything at that time.

When he leaned back in, and felt that cold steel on the barber chair, that creature took my twelve-year-old hand and very quietly told me to put my hand back on the arm of that chair. He then proceeded to place his penis back on my hand. I don't know if the men in the shop could see what was happening or not.

My father and brother were at the front of the shop, and I was near the back. This man was someone my father would have had no problem with, which is why I was having my hair cut by him. My twelve-year-old mind was screaming inside! I was petrified! When he finished my hair, with a look of satisfaction on his lecherous face, he handed me the mirror to check the cut. I did, and I got up and went and told my father what happened. Thank God, my mouth was released! I was not going to cover up for another pedophile. Well, my father went off! He confronted the man and he lied about it all. After that, we never saw that man at that shop again. It is a miracle that my father didn't beat the man to death. Yet, I continued emotional eating and gaining weight.

By the time I entered middle school, I was 5'6½" and weighed 205 pounds. I had such an awakening because the kids I had gone to elementary and middle school with were now in the seventh and eighth grades, and they looked like grown men and women to me. The difference with the girls is that they were sizes 5, 7 and 9, and I was all of a size 16 and 18. I was an overweight, adolescent female who had officially become obese.

Childhood obesity is not, and never has been, an issue to take lightly. It is serious business, and I have devoted a good portion of my life researching and advocating for overweight and obese adolescent girls and women who have been sexually assaulted during their childhood. It is a worthy cause. One of my ministry focuses is to champion the cause and deliverance for hurting girls and women, to see them become transformed by the renewing of their minds. To first present their minds, bodies and souls as a living sacrifice, holy and acceptable to God; this is our reasonable service, as shared in Romans 12:1-2 (KJV). The elaboration on the sacredness of our temple is a worthy topic to discuss.

Mental and Emotional Blockage

The human mind, and its capacity, is amazing to me. For in our minds lays the ability for humans to "do and be." We are what we think we are, and we become what we mindfully conceptualize ourselves to be. When it comes to issues of trauma and fear, the human mind oftentimes switches itself into survival mode and represses the memory as a safeguard. However, with regard to this phase of my life, I actively and effectively blocked it out of my mind for a period of time. Twenty-five years to be exact.

During the years of my not remembering the molestation, periodically, I would have a flashback to the incident. It would scare me, and I would will it back to the dark region of my mind, thereby, not remembering or being conscious of the assault. When I look back over those times, I have often wondered if that was the way God was encouraging me to deal with the pain of it all. Each time, I could not, and would not, deal with it during my childhood, adolescent and young adult years.

Later in my life, as I eventually tried to deal with the memories of the molestation, God spoke to me through dreams, visions and revelations. I experienced the power of

God moving me in a direction that eventually involved me ministering to women and girls about my life, with full transparency. The heaviness of sexual assault of any kind had to be dealt with. I am an ordained minister and pastor. The residual effects of CSA began to come to the surface, and I could no longer push the memories to the darkness of not remembering. There was work for me to do and victims of CSA for me to minister and administer to. The act of sweeping it under the rug and acting as if the victim was in the wrong, had to be addressed from the standpoint and viewpoint of women who are in the church. I have found that many women are hurting and bleeding in their spirits right there in the church; this can no longer be dismissed.

The number of women and men who have died with the memory of sexual assault, those who have committed suicide because of the shame of it and having blamed themselves for the heinous acts of sick individuals, and those who have turned to prostitution, promiscuity, repeated the act on others. They closed themselves off to the possibility of loving relationships. This is alarming. The effects of sexual assault are damaging and must be dealt with for the deliverance of mankind.

I could go on and on about my plight with food, as well as the internal, psychological and spiritual issues that complicated my life. All of these issues combined didn't make me feel as good as I should have during my teenage years and my young adult years. I had low self-esteem issues. I tried to hide this by throwing myself into school, work and church activities. But there always came a time when being the "big girl" in the group made a difference, especially as I became a teenager and wanted to date boys. The heavier I became, the less the boys were looking at me as a possible girlfriend or to date. They were looking at the smaller girls who had confidence and presented themselves as datable. I was too many times the sisterly one. This state of being affected me in so many ways. I needed healing.

At age 33, I could no longer deny what had happened. I told my family and the man that I was dating about the first molestation. The confession was cathartic for me. I felt free to move forward with my life and to begin to effectively develop a healthy lifestyle and lose not only the emotional weight, but the physical weight, as well. I've had to unlearn many bad habits that I'd developed, and I realize several years later that I am a work in progress. I am no longer bound by the sexual assaults and that has come from a life dedicated to prayer and a desire to be whole. In addition, I have forgiven both men who violated me for what they did to me. I had to do it to become totally free within.

If you are indecisive about speaking up about sexual assault, please surround yourself with a positive support system that can help you. I had to learn to apply the advice I've written in this chapter by first opening my mind and accepting that my small scope of reference—that was filled with fear—needed to be enlarged. I had to move on to the bigger picture—to see universally and to walk in that new understanding. There are no limits. Now I burn proverbial boxes and refuse to be labeled or classified based on what others think about me. I move by another standard—one of freedom and liberation, and I pray the same for you.

Breaking the Cycle of Silence
Reflection Questions

1. Victims of sexual abuse, at any age, are so often pensive about coming forward to talk with counselors, therapists, spiritual leaders and coaches who want to help them in their healing. How can we encourage them to begin the healing process and encourage relationship counseling?

    _____

    _____

    _____

    _____

    _____

2. Overweight and obesity is a global public health pandemic, affecting much of our world. Our children need attention and consistency with this issue. What steps can we take within our families to promote and maintain healthy living?

    _____

    _____

    _____

    _____

    _____

3. Childhood sexual abuse and obesity are major, compounded issues. Healing is necessary. In addition to counseling and therapy, what other steps can we take to move toward successful changes for victims?

_____

_____

_____

_____

_____

ABOUT THE AUTHOR

Tracey Booker

Rev. Tracey Booker is President and CEO of Tracey Booker Enterprises, a lifestyle development company. She is also the Executive Director of Metamorphosis, Incorporated, a faith-based, female-oriented service organization that empowers women and girls through various life changes and transitions. Tracey is pursuing a PhD in Human and Social Services and has attained a Master of Science degree in Counseling: Studies in Human Behavior, and a Bachelor of Arts in Communications: Radio, Television and Film.

Rev. Booker currently serves as the pastor of Triumph the Church and Kingdom of God in Christ, in Oak Ridge, North Carolina. She currently serves as the General Secretary for Church Advancement for the international church organization.

An internationally published author, noted inspirational and motivational speaker and podcast personality, Rev. Booker has a commitment to making positive change. She has dedicated her life to helping others by bringing a fresh, engaging approach for girls and women to dispel the feeling of victimization by their life circumstances. Through coaching and pastoral counseling, she encourages many to embrace the beauty in the reflection that shines in the mirror, in programs designed to be both conscientious and effective.

Director of Step to the Edge Coaching Transformational Life Coaching, she calls awareness to the innate power to change lives through transformation and a change of mindset. Her coaching method centers on the conversion of the mind, transfiguration, change and movement to the next level of greatness and mastery, which begins with the renewing of the mind.

For more information, visit www.traceybooker.com or email info@traceybooker.com.

ABOUT

So It Is Written

 We help entrepreneurs write the ONE book that will expand their reach and get them to SIX figures in record time! Period!

As the leading content curators for six-figure authorpreneurs and entrepreneurs, So It Is Written is best known for helping them package and leverage their expertise into a bestselling book, which amplifies their brand, accelerates their paydays and attracts bigger opportunities!

Let us help you brand in excellence as an author and entrepreneur so you can develop multiple streams of income from just ONE book!

Call us at 313-777-8607 today or email info@soitiswritten.net for more details about our services. We look forward to working with you to make your project one of excellence!